This book is a marvellous contribution to the emerging field of team coaching. Dr Stout-Rostron and her contributing authors have produced a review of extant team coaching models and contributed some new models for team coaching specifically aimed at respecting and capitalising on the cultural diversity found in today's modern workplace. Much of the work undertaken here seeks to move beyond the linear models that have characterised coaching in past years. Instead, they explore systemic and developmental approaches to team coaching. In doing so, they contribute to a more sophisticated understanding of team coaching and coaching more generally. This is a book which is both theoretically strong and practically applicable. I am sure it will enhance practice and stimulate further development in this important area of coaching.

—**Dr Michael Cavanagh,** *Deputy Director, Coaching Psychology Unit, University of Sydney, Australia*

Team coaching is increasingly popular and credible as the people-development approach for businesses navigating the complex demands impacting on today's workplace. We can no longer ignore the global platform of this digital age, further compounded by the unprecedented cultural mix in team composition. This seminal text, contextualised in relationship systems intelligence, offers expertise and knowledge that prepares and elevates your offering as a team coach. You can develop and distinguish your practice, informed by proven interventions implemented by successful practitioners. Current case studies from a range of sectors are reinforced with tangible illustrations and a range of team coaching models. You will be taken on a journey of discovery into every facet of team coaching – transformational leadership, a systemic perspective on culture and human relationships, and differentiation between group and team coaching. A text that I highly recommend you view as a must-have reference in all your preparations for team coaching.

—**Dr Lise Lewis,** *International Special Ambassador, European Mentoring and Coaching Council (EMCC), London, UK*

In this timely and useful book, the authors draw on their considerable experience and address key concerns and approaches to team coaching, stressing the importance of culture and the role that diversity plays in the process. Systems Theory is fast emerging as the dominant

discourse for coaching in organisations, and the models offered here do well to expose its importance. Highly recommended reading for coaches working with teams.

—**Dr Marc Kahn,** *Global Head of HR and OD, Investec Plc; Visiting Professor of People, Organisation and Strategy, Middlesex University, London, UK*

Sunny has this knack. As a top researcher and coaching professional she sees. And then she digs. And then she confirms. And then she writes, giving us the gift of seeing, too. And soon rumblings and shiftings and leapings become the norm, and the world is different. Her latest book does all of that again, and on probably the most important issue of our time: cultural difference. If you transform your team along Sunny's lines (and that of her very able colleagues), you will, I am sure, feel the gratitude to her that I feel every day. Our differences are music. This book makes sure we build a symphony every time we meet, every time we think together, every time we decide, every time we act. And soon we cannot un-see this sonorous reality ever again. It becomes our own wisdom.

—**Nancy Kline,** *Time to Think, Inc.; author of* Time to Think *and* More Time to Think

This is a much-needed book in the coaching world. It provides an overview of many team coaching models, summarising the key components and sharing the frameworks, as well as demonstrating techniques within each model. In this way it serves as a text book or resource book. The wealth of knowledge contained in this book makes it a "Must Read", and it is an essential integrated guide to best practices in team coaching. The sharing of theory supported by case studies provides a solid bridge between theoretical understanding and practical implementation. The contributing authors add a diversity and richness to a gem of a book. Highly recommended for coaches wanting to transition to team coaching, but equally valuable to existing practitioners in team coaching. Leaders, HR and talent managers, and those who want to generate higher sustainable performance within their teams will also benefit from reading this book.

—**Dr Natalie Cunningham,** *Executive Board Member, Graduate School Alliance Education Coaching; Research Associate, Gordon Institute of Business Science, University of Pretoria, South Africa*

A powerful guide to lead and leverage the value of diverse teams through coaching. It provides the inspiration, wisdom and tools for leaders and teams to thrive in dynamic, culturally diverse global environments.

—**Jeanett Modise,** *Chief HR Officer, Sanlam Investments, Cape Town, South Africa*

This book clearly lays out the best approach to improving team performance. With clear practical case studies, the author guides and highlights the many real situations one faces in the corporate world. Managing teams and learning how best to identify skills and talents among your different personalities must be one of the greatest challenges to corporate harmony. Furthermore, the book gives clear guidelines on how to handle conflict and navigate change, and most importantly on how to apportion responsibilities. This book is an all-in-one easy guide to improving the productivity of your key players.

—**Suzanne Ackerman-Berman,** *Transformation Director, Pick n Pay, South Africa*

This book is a well-researched synthesis of contemporary literature on group and team coaching, woven together with evidence from recent organisational case studies and the author's own extraordinary insights. As an immensely practical go-to-guide for any professional in the leadership development space working with teams and seeking to build requisite leadership team capability for any organisation to thrive in a complex, culturally diverse world, this is a must-read!

—**Sandri van Wyk,** *Chief Advisor Leadership Development, Human Resources, Eskom, South Africa*

The book includes practical cases and an introduction to the latest team coaching approaches. You will find relevant concepts of team coaching, and how to cope with the challenges of the technological revolution, starting with the effective and robust concept of transformative leadership, together with approaches for transforming organisational cultures and even on management of diversity and culture in modern international teams. Have you ever heard of Ubuntu Coaching? Certainly not, but if you read the special chapter, like me, you can learn from African practices how to use a very pragmatic transcultural approach to working on themes in teams. In addition, you will find a concept of Relationship Systems Coaching and a High-Performance Relationship Coaching Model. You will not find a more comprehensive integration of individual and team coaching. Sunny is completely right in her conclusion that "the core competence we are working with in team coaching is that of learning – and the learning must always start with the coach". I will use her book for my coach training. I am sure that this inspiring book is needed by the field for visionary and integrated team coaching!

—**Prof Dr Siegfried Greif,** *University of Osnabrück, Work and Organisational Psychology Unit, and Institut für psychologische Forschung und Beratung GmbH (IwFB) (Institute of Business Psychological Research and Counselling), Germany*

By having in mind the rapid changes in our organisational culture and the transformational impact of technology, the authors of this book successfully emphasise the necessity of a collaborative approach relevant to our working environment. The best way to grasp the spirit of this book is by referring to African Ubuntu philosophy that grasps the essence of being human. It literally means that a person is a person through other people. It embraces hospitality, caring about others, and being willing to go the extra mile for the sake of another. As Nelson Mandela said, Ubuntu is a vital instrument to "bridge the gaps between people in the workplace, stakeholders within and outside the enterprise and business and the broader society in which they operate". This perspective on team coaching is the best testimonial and gift that an African-based book can give to the world.

—**Dr Reinhard Stelter,** *Professor of Coaching Psychology, University of Copenhagen; Visiting Professor, Copenhagen Business School, Denmark*

Team coaching is an area of growing interest, and every effort at a detailed review of experience in delivering these interventions is an important contribution for everyone who cares about the way people work in organisations. Practitioners looking for guidance in this developing field of knowledge will find in this book a wealth of ideas from those who can be trusted. The authors have made useful and thoughtful links between what other disciplines have been working on, and what coaching thought leaders are currently conceptualising. This book also stands out from others as it brings the topic of diversity of participants into the very focus of team coaching; an increasingly prominent feature of our life in organisations.

—**Professor Tatiana Bachkirova,** *Director, International Centre for Coaching and Mentoring Studies at Oxford Brookes University, UK*

The authors provide a useful introduction for practitioners who work with global teams in today's diverse world.

—**Dr David Drake,** *CEO, Moment Institute, San Francisco, California, USA*

Transformational Coaching to Lead Culturally Diverse Teams

In this book, Dr Sunny Stout-Rostron examines real-world experience and the contemporary literature on group and team coaching. She analyses how team coaching can guide coaches to help leaders and teams flourish in complex, culturally diverse organisations. As well as presenting a variety of team coaching models, she also presents her own model, High-Performance Relationship Coaching, the result of many years of working with global corporate teams.

Dr Stout-Rostron illuminates how team coaches can help teams to learn from and interpret their own experiences, and to understand the complexity of the environment in which they work. Her team coaching model is explored over eight chapters, beginning with the role of the business team coach and leadership coaching processes. She evaluates how to work in the Fourth Industrial Revolution and how to shift culture through transformative leadership coaching, explains the depth of relationship systems coaching and explores how to apply a variety of methods including Ubuntu coaching. The book encourages team coaches to develop deep self-awareness, team awareness, cultural diversity awareness and wider systemic and relationship awareness. Filled with practical stories and examples, it describes how to work successfully with these models in the real world.

Transformational Coaching to Lead Culturally Diverse Teams is a key guide for coaches in practice and in training, HR and L&D professionals and executives in a coaching role. This is essential reading for all team coaches.

Sunny Stout-Rostron is founder of Sunny Stout-Rostron Associates CC, a founding Director of People Quotient (Pty) Ltd, an Advisory Board Director with the Professional Development Foundation UK (PDF), a Founding Fellow and Research Advisor at the Institute of Coaching at McLean Hospital (a Harvard Medical School Affiliate) and Founding President of Coaches and Mentors of South Africa (COMENSA). Stout-Rostron coaches internationally.

Routledge Focus on Coaching

The Focus on Coaching series features books which cover an aspect of coaching particularly dear to the author's or editor's heart that they wish to share with the wider professional coaching community. The series editors are Windy Dryden and David A. Lane.

Titles in the series:

The Coaching Alliance
Theory and Guidelines for Practice
Windy Dryden

A Practical Guide to Rational Emotive Behavioural Coaching
Windy Dryden

Resilience as a Framework for Coaching
A Cognitive Behavioural Perspective
Michael Neenan

Transformational Coaching to Lead Culturally Diverse Teams
Edited by Sunny Stout-Rostron

For a full list of titles in this series, please visit https://www.routledge.com/Routledge-Focus-on-Coaching/book-series/RFC

Transformational Coaching to Lead Culturally Diverse Teams

Edited by Sunny Stout-Rostron

LONDON AND NEW YORK

First published 2019 by Routledge

2 Park Square, Milton Park, Abingdon, Oxfordshire OX14 4RN
52 Vanderbilt Avenue, New York, NY 10017

Routledge is an imprint of the Taylor & Francis Group, an informa business

First issued in paperback 2020

British Library Cataloguing-in-Publication Data
A catalogue record for this book is available from the British Library

Library of Congress Cataloging-in-Publication Data
Names: Stout-Rostron, Sunny, author.
Title: Transformational coaching to lead culturally diverse teams / Sunny Stout-Rostron.
Description: Abingdon, Oxon; New York, NY: Routledge, 2019. | Series: Routledge focus on coaching
Identifiers: LCCN 2018051614 (print) | LCCN 2018053063 (ebook) | ISBN 9780429465741 (Master eBook) | ISBN 9780429879531 (Mobipocket) | ISBN 9780429879555 (Abode Reader) | ISBN 9781138610507 (hardback)
Subjects: LCSH: Teams in the workplace—Management. | Employees—Coaching of. | Diversity in the workplace—Management. | Leadership.
Classification: LCC HD66 (ebook) | LCC HD66 .R675 2019 (print) | DDC 658.4/02208—dc23
LC record available at https://lccn.loc.gov/2018051614

ISBN: 978-1-138-61050-7 (hbk)
ISBN: 978-0-367-60655-8 (pbk)

Typeset in Times New Roman
by codeMantra

With thanks to Wendy Johnson, CEO of the Worldwide Association of Business Coaches (WABC), a tireless champion of our profession.

—Sunny Stout-Rostron, Cape Town, July 2018

Contents

Figures

Contributors

Dumisani Magadlela, PhD, is a behavioural scientist, certified international executive coach and leadership development facilitator based in Johannesburg, South Africa. Dumi uses emotional intelligence and Ubuntu principles and practices to ignite human excellence within individual and organisational systems. He has been helping organisations develop dynamic and high-performance cultures for many years, focusing on individual and collective leadership behaviours and values. He serves on the faculty of The Coaching Centre in Cape Town where he teaches coaching, leadership, culture change and Ubuntu awareness. Dumi works across the African continent and has recently co-edited a pioneering journal on African coaching and consulting.

Anne Rød, MA, is an international management consultant and executive team coach who develops and delivers team development and leadership programmes for global organisations. Through her work, Anne swiftly assesses and refocuses the strategic requirements of challenging leadership situations. A senior faculty member with CRR Global, Anne spearheads Relationship Systems Intelligence™ training in organisations and management teams around the world. In 2003, she published a textbook on organisational communication (*Informasjon & Samfunnskontakt – en innføring*), and recently published a white paper with Marita Fridjhon and Faith Fuller on Relationship Systems Intelligence™ and Systems-Inspired Leadership™. Anne lives with her family in Oslo.

Creina Schneier, MBA BA (Hons) Ind & Org Psy, BSocSci, works systemically with individuals and teams to build a culture that encourages and supports the best from those within it; this is what drives and delights Creina in her practice. She believes that sustainable organisational performance improvement can be achieved through heightened awareness, robust engagement, greater alignment, deeper collaboration and more effective communication. Professionally, she thrives on partnering leaders to build intelligent teams and thinking environments. Creina has over 20 years' experience in the field of change leadership and leadership and organisational development. Her work has included working individually with leaders, large-scale leadership transformation, leadership capacity building and team coaching.

Sunny Stout-Rostron, DProf MA, coaches at senior executive and board levels. She has a wide range of experience in leadership development, helping organisations cultivate collaborative strategies to manage relationship systems, culture change and conflict. Sunny has played a leading role in building the profession of coaching and has created a succession of leadership and management programmes in the corporate, legal and educational fields. Her passion is to deepen the knowledge base for coaching through research and critical reflective practice, as well as fostering an understanding and implementation of genuine cultural diversity in organisations. Sunny is a Doctoral Supervisor at several business schools and is a member of the Management Coaching faculty of the School of Business at the University of Stellenbosch, and on the Global Faculty of Time to Think Inc. She is also a Founding Fellow of the Institute of Coaching at McLean Hospital, a Harvard Medical School Affiliate, Founding President of Coaches and Mentors of South Africa (COMENSA) and a long-standing member of the Worldwide Association of Business Coaches. Sunny is the author of six books including *Leadership Coaching for Results: Cutting-Edge Practices for Coach and Client* (Knowres, 2014), *Business Coaching International: Transforming Individuals and Organisations* (Karnac 2009/2013) and *Business Coaching Wisdom and Practice: Unlocking the Secrets of Business Coaching* (Knowres, 2009/2012).

Deborah Williams, MPhil, is a human capital specialist in organisational development and leadership. She holds a Master of Philosophy in Management Coaching from the University of Stellenbosch. After 12 years as MD of a highly successful training company, she moved into the role of Head of Learning and Development and Organisational Design at Metropolitan Health. In her current role as an Organisational Development consultant, she sits on the ExCo of the Human Capital Department of the Health Division of MMI Holdings and drives leadership interventions and coaching in the Division. Her passion is transforming leadership to create an enabling culture and optimise team engagement and performance.

1 Introduction

Team coaching

Sunny Stout-Rostron

The business issues facing us today need innovative thinking and fresh solutions, and so cannot be solved by one inspired leader, but by interconnected teams that are having to adapt to changing societies and cultures. This requires pioneering new organisational processes and strategies – and vitally, harnessing the technological-digital Fourth Industrial Revolution. To do so, organisations are increasingly looking to team-based working units to improve agility, organisational flexibility and competitiveness.

What does a business team coach do?

Team coaching focuses on an effective, sustainable and measurable way of developing managerial leaders and their teams. A business team coach encourages clients to think for themselves and to develop an awareness of their own conscious and unconscious behaviours, which may influence performance in the workplace. Traditionally, the development of organisations and corporations supported business and performance development models, but ignored the importance of values to individuals, teams and the business – which underpin organisational culture and behaviours. This crucial lack laid the foundation for the development of individual and team coaching – not just for leaders and senior executives but for individuals at all levels within the workforce.

For this reason, organisations have integrated team-based structures into their daily organisational routine. Although "team" and "group" are often mentioned simultaneously, they differ in terms of their interdependence. Individuals within a group tend to work independently with minimal mutual accountability, whereas a team member has individual and collective accountability while working independently and interdependently (Abrahamson, 2016: 8).

Team-based work units allow for a move from the model of the dominating single leader to a collective leadership model where team members can step into multiple roles and functions (Abrahamson, 2016: 12). Inside this new environment, the role of the team coach is to help individuals to find their own voice, and yet help the team to create its own collective and supportive processes to achieve organisational outcomes.

The team coach helps the team to learn from and interpret their own experiences, and to understand the complexity of the environment in which they work. Team coaching works because it is about the results experienced through the relationship between the coach, each individual and the resulting team dynamic. It is from this base that the team continues to build their relationships with key stakeholders within the business – it is critical that the team identifies all the relationships that are core to the business. Gaps are identified in terms of building relationships, managing people, problem solving, decision-making, executing strategy, communication skills and facilitating meetings. The team will work together in alignment with organisational values and goals.

This book examines the contemporary literature on group and team coaching to see how it can guide coaches to help leaders and teams manage and flourish in complex, culturally diverse organisations and societies. It introduces a variety of team coaching models, culminating in the author's team coaching model which is the result of numerous case studies over many years working with global corporate teams. This model, developed through organisational team coaching practice, includes deeper development of self-awareness, team awareness, diversity awareness, cultural awareness and wider systemic and relationship awareness. The book provides coaching stories and examples to highlight how to work with the models and tools being presented.

My work has been strongly influenced by the need in South Africa for coaches and leaders to learn to manage diversity, develop cultural competence, understand leadership as a function of cultural difference and develop an ability to lead and coach across cultures. As a British-American, I continue to coach in the United States, as well as in the United Kingdom, Europe and Australia and across sub-Saharan Africa. I believe that successful management of today's increasingly diverse workforce is one of the most important global challenges faced by all leaders. The move from homogeneous to heterogeneous societies is an irreversible trend, and many of today's organisational challenges stem from the inability of leaders to fully comprehend the dynamics of diversity and culture.

Contributing authors

This book represents my personal, signature approach to team coaching along with that of my four contributors: Deborah Williams, Dr Dumisani Magadlela, Creina Schneier and Anne Rød. My coaching work over the last decade has been strongly influenced by the Thinking Environment®, Relationship Systems Intelligence™ and Systemic Team Coaching (STC). Also, as I live and work in South Africa, much of my last two decades in organisational work and research has been focused on culture and diversity. Research suggests that cultural diversity in the workplace has significant potential to enhance business success (Stout-Rostron, 2017). It is therefore important that business coaches working in a global marketplace understand diversity and develop an understanding of the multicultural issues facing coaches and their coachees on a daily basis.

What is clear to us in our approach to team and individual coaching is that we partner with the client, become trusted advisors and help them to become trusted advisors to their stakeholders. We tend to work experientially, collaborate extensively within the client's system and collaborate externally with other executive and team coaches to be sure that we are designing the right programme and bringing in the best coaches for the intervention.

It is not our approach to be the expert, be directive or pretend that we have the answers for our clients. Our aim is to help the team members to develop their own thinking, feelings, appropriate behaviours and outcomes when considering their new challenges. The team coach is a catalyst in helping the team to generate new thinking.

Aim of the book

Our aim is to introduce you – whether leader, coach or Human Resources (HR)/Organisational Development consultant – to current thinking on coaching teams and the variety of models available to you so that you can develop and begin to practise working with your own team coaching model. We bring to you a practical and experiential book with theories and tools which you can apply immediately to your own team coaching.

To gain the most wisdom from the experience of other team coaches, my four contributing authors share with you their expertise in working with teams across a wide variety of global sectors. Creina Schneier and Anne Rød explain the nuts and bolts of Relationship Systems Intelligence and Relationship Systems Coaching. Deborah Williams shares her experience as an internal Organisational Development consultant within the field of financial insurance and medical administration, who also works in partnership with a variety of external team coaches. Dumisani Magadlela introduces us to the African concept of Ubuntu and its practical application and relevance to global teams.

Client stories: teams A, B and C

This section introduces three client teams in different organisations and the journey they set out on for their team coaching. We bring in various stories throughout the book as the teams progress on their journeys. For the purposes of confidentiality, organisational names and details have been omitted.

Team A – Human Resources ExCo for financial services company

- Initial meetings with stakeholders.
- Draft proposal.
- Design of the individual and team coaching interventions.
- Individual coaching interviews.
- Emergent themes document.
- Meetings with sponsors.
- Management and leadership individual and team profiles.
- Two-day initial team inauguration forum.
- Ten monthly half-day team coaching sessions.
- Interim regular reviews and final closing review.

Team A was an HR ExCo comprising 18 team members within a financial services company. The brief was to work with team coaching as a way of developing the HR ExCo's performance, effectiveness and ability to manage change. The process involved several initial meetings with the Strategic HR Director. Based on our discussions, we designed a team coaching intervention that would be practical and experiential – helping team members to work from their own experience to learn how to better manage themselves and lead others. Our focus was building relationships, being authentic communicators, engaging positively with each other, and managing how to structure and facilitate meetings at every level in the business.

This was a very diverse team in terms of race, gender, experience and expertise. The overarching brief was to develop leadership capacity, trust, accountability and the ability to manage conflict, broadening out the team's influence and visibility within the larger organisation.

Team coaching process

To commence the process, I put in a proposal with clearly identified stages which would be reviewed as we completed each stage. My initial meetings were with the sponsors and leaders in the team coaching process. Together we designed a draft proposal for the entire intervention. I then met with each team member in individual 75-minute sessions to get to know them and understand their roles and responsibilities. This allowed me time to build trust and rapport while gaining an understanding of the organisational culture – and what was working and not working within the team.

The next step was to sit in on one of the ExCo meetings to observe how they communicated and engaged with each other. This gave me an idea of how meetings were facilitated, the levels of conflict, how that was managed, who spoke up in meetings and who remained silent or disengaged. Armed with all this information, we agreed to hold a two-day team inauguration forum away from the office, which was to lay the building blocks for our team coaching sessions. Prior to this, each participant completed a leadership profile we planned to use during the two-day forum to help develop individual self-awareness and team relationship awareness.

In the two-day forum, we began to work with the specific behaviours required for team success and to identify the core issues helping or hindering the team's performance. We worked with specific issues that needed to be addressed, at the same time as building relationships, forging new ways of working and bonding as a team that could begin to work with more trust and safety. We identified how the team wished to work in future. My role was to facilitate this through the subsequent monthly team coaching sessions. The purpose of the two-day forum was to build the skills and behaviours to enable better communication and engagement with each other. This also formed the basis of our team coaching sessions together.

A month after the team inauguration forum, we commenced regular monthly team coaching sessions for a period of ten months. With my two sponsors, we incorporated a review every third month to identify new behaviours, new learning and enhanced performance within the team. Each monthly team coaching session was designed in the light of issues emerging within the team and core events taking place within the business, and in alignment with the team and organisational strategy. Throughout the entire process, I had regular meetings with my sponsors including the Head of Strategic HR to keep us on track with organisational as well as team goals. Towards the end of the process, we had a final review of what learnings had emerged from the overall process.

Team B – Business Unit ExCo for medical scheme administrator

- Initial meetings with stakeholders.
- Draft proposal.
- Design of the individual and team coaching interventions.
- Individual coaching interviews.
- Emergent themes document.
- Meetings with sponsors.
- Management and leadership profiles.
- Two-day initial team inauguration forum.
- Ten monthly half-day team coaching sessions.
- Interim regular reviews and final closing review.

Client challenges

Team B was my case study to continue to develop and test my team coaching model. I worked with colleagues who were also completing their International STC Senior Practitioner Diploma with Peter Hawkins and John Leary-Joyce. It was a requirement to take on a team coaching assignment with a real team in an external organisation for a period of 12 months. The team coaching assignment was to run in parallel with the STC modular programme, giving the team coaches a chance to apply their learning from each module throughout the life of the programme. I and my co-team coach worked with the Hawkins' STC Model, which encompasses CID-CLEAR and the Five Disciplines of *commissioning, clarifying, co-creating, connecting* and *core learning*. Through working with this team coaching model, and integrating it with the way I had been working with teams for years, my own coaching model emerged.

This Business Unit, part of a larger company, was carrying out the administration work for an external client, a large medical scheme. The Unit was facing the challenge of retention of client and service excellence which required a shift in leadership focus. I was asked to work with a team which combined the ExCo leaders of the Business Unit and the senior managers within the larger company. The decision was to employ an external coach who understood the culture and business of the larger corporate group and who could work with the ExCo of the smaller Business Unit to be sure they strengthened delivery to the client going forward.

The organisation wanted a successful team and individual coaching intervention for the Business Unit, where members of the team would begin to step into their leadership roles in a more powerful, visible and sustainable way – in order to become a more high-performing and learning team. The focus was on building leadership capacity, managing diverse teams more effectively, building a healthy relationship with the core client and becoming more mature and effective leaders within the business overall.

During this 18-month process, there were two major restructurings within the overarching business. As a result, there were significant systemic hurdles to deal with at each stage of the project.

Team coaching process

There was a considerable tumult during the first eight months. As a result of the two major restructurings, at every team session someone had been removed from the team due to resignations or moving to new roles or appointments, and new members had been added. Also, after seven months of team coaching, the Business Unit changed from one senior leader to two senior leaders – one responsible for integration and operations, and the other for client relationship management. At this point, we also identified a need to work closely with the newly appointed CEO of the Business Unit – another change. The constant reformations of the team meant a continual forming, storming, norming and performing throughout the entire contract. This posed a great challenge for the two team coaches and for the team itself.

Throughout the team and individual coaching process with this client, I formed a strong partnership with the then Head of L&D and Organisational Development, Deborah Williams, who worked with me as my co-team coach. We were jointly overseen by the Divisional Human Capital Executive, who signed off on this project (which was initiated by Deborah). I made sure to be in coach supervision with an external coach supervisor for the entire project and learned the value of working with a co-facilitator who was an internal member of the organisation. She was always present to help navigate the complex matrix structure of the company. Together we have grown as team coaches, and I would always advocate working with a co-facilitator, as you can take the team further and deeper than when simply working on your own.

The process was slightly different to Team A's process, as I was deliberately learning the STC Model and looking to integrate my learnings into the way I was working. I will describe the workings of the STC Model in Chapter 4 to give you a broad concept of how to work with it.

Team C – IT company ExCo and staff

- Initial meetings with ExCo.
- Draft team coaching proposal.
- Individual ExCo coaching interviews.
- Emergent themes document and report-back to ExCo.
- Individual staff coaching interviews.
- Emergent themes document and 360° feedback session to ExCo and staff.
- Design of the overarching team coaching interventions.
- Two-day initial team inauguration forum.
- Four monthly half-day team coaching sessions.
- Intermittent ExCo follow-up conversations.
- Values and behaviours organisational survey.
- Values and behaviours survey report.
- Fifth team coaching session – designing organisational values and behaviours.

On this project, I worked with a co-facilitator, Creina Schneier. Our IT client company was established during the early 2000s out of an extended project in which the MD was engaged. The MD invited a second consultant to join him, and together they built a successful IT consultancy. Although growth was slow at first, the small initial staff complement has grown in recent years to a total of more than 20, including four full-time directors, three senior managers and an Executive Chair. Growth has brought an inevitable increase in complexity and a need for organisational structures and operating systems, such as financial and HR systems – as much as "soft systems" that address management and leadership within the business.

Client challenges

The directors acknowledged their relative lack of leadership and management expertise. They expressed a shared desire to "do the right thing" that manifests in many ways, including "wanting to contribute to the development of the country" and "produce quality work on time", and in the workplace a wish to lead, manage and develop staff properly.

Team coaching process

Team C was a different experience as we were working with a smaller business. Creina and I worked as consultants and co-team coaches during the ten-month process. We first met with the eight-member

ExCo to ascertain whether there was resonance in the potential relationship and to gain an understanding of what they believed to be their major issue – that is, a lack of management and leadership skills, as the senior leaders were primarily technical experts. The eight-member ExCo were passionate about their business but were experiencing serious conflicts with each other and with their staff. There were diversity and gender issues, and the staff had become increasingly vocal as the company grew.

Creina and I facilitated a Leadership ExCo 360° feedback session based on our initial interviews with the eight-member ExCo. One month later, we interviewed the entire staff and facilitated a Staff 360° feedback session in conjunction with the ExCo. The original purpose of the coaching interviews was to provide clarity on the leaders' job roles, to have them articulate what was and what was not working for them and to identify how the senior leaders saw their core strengths and areas for development. The second stage of coaching interviews, with the staff, was designed to collect relevant data and impressions the staff held about the leadership team and organisational culture. This provided a chance for the staff to share their perceptions of the company culture and relationship system. An additional aim was to allow time for the leaders and staff to develop trust with each other, as well as a relationship with the coaches. The primary purpose of the interviews and feedback sessions, which were conducted like team coaching processes, was for the coaches to more deeply understand the organisational environment and company climate. A further purpose was to understand the organisation's current functioning, the aspirations of both leaders and staff for the company overall, and to identify what were the individual and team coaching needs within the organisation.

We facilitated a two-day team inauguration forum with the ExCo and five subsequent half-day team coaching sessions. Our learning from this process was that it was not complete. We needed at least two more team coaching sessions, but budgetary constraints also had to be taken into consideration. My co-team coach and I learned a major lesson – when we truly understand what might be needed for a team, we should ensure that we do everything possible to be able to complete the process. As it happened, we closed the loop with a final session preceded by a values and behaviours survey and a concluding team coaching workshop to help the organisation to design their values and underpinning behaviours going forward. In the future, we may go back to work with this small IT company. In the meantime, they have learned new management skills, developed leadership capacity and begun to understand and work with the cultural diversity in the organisation. The next stage of our process with this team is in individual coaching sessions, which will help them develop the cultural competence they need to be effective leaders.

Leadership coaching approaches

Throughout the three organisational coaching interventions, my co-coaches and I were able to bring what is considered "cutting-edge" coaching approaches and methodologies to our clients in a way that directly addressed client needs. In these instances, we suggested approaches underpinned primarily by Systems-Inspired Leadership™, creating a Thinking Environment and developing cultural competence.

Systems-Inspired Leadership

Systems-Inspired Leadership is an advanced and courageous way of approaching leadership and team interactions. The development of Systems-Inspired Leadership in a team or organisational system helps accelerate mind-and-heart-sets that are needed to face the challenges of this millennium. It equips leaders, teams and organisations with a mental model to access, align and lead people to higher performance. This offers unlimited possibilities in terms of awareness, maturity, creativity, choice, leadership and collaboration. By redirecting the focus from individuals in the system to the system as an entity in itself, Systems-Inspired Leadership enables leaders and teams to tap into the true potential of human beings in action.

Systems-Inspired Leadership catalyses the ability of leaders, teams and organisations to move beyond personal concerns to a powerful and positive group identity with resilience and resources to address the challenges ahead. It enables leaders to grasp increased levels of mental complexity, identify patterns of interdependence and lead the necessary paradigm shifts to take the organisation into the future.

Systems-Inspired Leadership respectfully involves the creativity and intelligence in the organisation to co-design and drive the process going forward. Our approach brings people together to create an environment and culture where constructive interaction leads to a shared understanding from which common goals are developed. When Systems-Inspired Leadership is combined with the creation of a Thinking Environment, a team is enabled to tap into their inherent knowledge, creativity and capability, to move from success to success, and to embrace the change that is the new normal.

Creating a Thinking Environment

> The quality of everything that human beings do depends on the quality of the thinking they do first. What more can we do to help people think for themselves?
>
> (Kline, 1999: 36)

The Thinking Environment is a practical way to put into action the values of *diversity* and *inclusiveness* throughout an organisation. Getting the best from people means getting their best thinking. This requires

> knowing how to treat people, how to offer them the highest-quality attention, how to ask incisive questions, how to recognise people's strengths and achievements, how to entice them beyond an addiction to certainty and into a preference for responsible risk.
>
> (Kline, personal communication, 10 May 2018)

A Thinking Environment is more efficient and more inclusive, and so leads to concrete positive business results. It produces high-quality ideas in less time and shows team members how to resolve difficulties more easily and to understand each other better – leaving them more enthusiastic about their work together, more hopeful of successes and with greater buy-in to decisions made by the group.

The Thinking Environment is a methodology developed by Nancy Kline, based on worldwide research into the behaviour of individuals, groups and organisations over a period of 40 years. These concepts evolved by engaging with issues of what best enables individuals and collectives to think effectively. In today's fast-paced times, true innovation, creativity and excellence can be found only if individuals are encouraged to think for themselves. Gone are the days when one or two people at the top of organisations could instruct others without their participation. Today, people want the freedom to contribute their unique skills and abilities to their organisations. Founded by Nancy Kline, the Thinking Environment is based on the premise that when individuals and groups learn to bring ten specific "behaviours" or "ways of being" together, they create an environment in which people can think beyond historic limiting assumptions towards greater creativity, power and effectiveness – thus achieving a higher level of personal, team and organisational performance.

Leading with cultural competence

Leaders and their teams are fast having to learn to manage diversity, develop cultural competence and understand leadership as a function of cultural difference. Sometimes, however, the problem is not isolated to one aspect of diversity but can cover a spectrum. Even in companies with fairly uniform ethnic or cultural homogeneity, there can be latent issues of gender, race, ethnicity, patriarchy and language.

Many current organisational challenges stem from the inability of leaders to fully comprehend the dynamics of diversity and culture. Their failure to dissociate themselves from their own biases and prejudices holds them back from giving free rein to the creativity and potential of a multicultural workforce. Cross-cultural research suggests that culture strongly influences leadership concepts, often in unconscious ways. Hence, the need for leaders to develop the necessary understanding and self-awareness to engage effectively with their teams and the issues involved.

Team-based work units allow for a move from the model of the unique single leader to a collective leadership model. Inside this new environment, the role of the team coach is to help individuals to find their own voice while helping the team to create its own collective and supportive processes to achieve organisational outcomes. In the rest of this book, we introduce you to the three processes with which we have worked in a variety of ways.

Systems-Inspired Leadership processes we have used are Relationship Systems Intelligence and Organisational Relationship Systems Coaching (ORSC™). We have integrated these processes with the Thinking Environment philosophy and processes, and brought in team coaching processes that also embody learning around cultural competence and leadership. As you read further, feel free to pick chapters that most resonate with you, and go back to those you have missed to fill in the gaps. We wish you an exciting journey in your learning as you continue to develop your own team coaching frameworks in conjunction with your clients.

References

Abrahamson, D. (2016). *Team Coaching: Why, Where, When and How*. WABC White Paper, Best Fit Business Coaching Series. Saanichton, BC: WABC Coaches.

Kline, N. (1999). *Time to Think: Listening to Ignite the Human Mind*. London: Cassell Illustrated.

2 Leadership and team coaching

Sunny Stout-Rostron

Working in the Fourth Industrial Revolution

Research shows that successful management of our increasingly diverse workforce is one of the most important global challenges faced by all leaders – at a time when we also face dizzying challenges from unimaginable advances in digital technology and artificial intelligence. It is important not only that leaders comprehend the dynamics of diversity and culture, but also that they grasp the dramatic transformation of society and organisations driven by the "Fourth Industrial Revolution".

In *The Future of the Professions: How Technology Will Transform the Work of Human Experts*, Susskind and Susskind (2015) predict the decline of today's professions, and raise important moral and ethical questions about people and the systems that will replace them. In a global internet age, they argue that our current professions are antiquated, impervious and no longer affordable. In an era when machines can outperform human beings at most tasks, they ask questions such as what are the prospects for employment, who should own and control online expertise and what tasks should be reserved exclusively for people? The authors argue how increasingly capable systems – from technology to artificial intelligence – are bringing lasting change to the ways in which the professional expertise of specialists is made available to society (Susskind and Susskind, 2015).

On the one hand, this upheaval may give voters the ability to challenge in unexpected ways the traditional powers of governments and institutions. On the other, the ordering and concentration of digital data poses threats to our privacy, presenting the potential of greater surveillance and control over citizens' lives. In addition, artificial intelligence will undoubtedly replace huge numbers of workers and professionals. As a result, the middle classes are more unsettled than at any time since the original Industrial Revolution. The idea of a secure job and steady career progress, guaranteed by professional qualifications or loyalty to one company, is fast receding. So, as a coach and as a leader, you need to stay at the forefront of learning and prepare your business or institution.

We are on the brink of a digital-technological transformation with a difference. It will fundamentally alter the way we live and work, yet we don't have any idea of how it will continue to unfold. We need to look at this as a phenomenon that will affect customer expectations, product enhancement, collaborative innovation and organisational and institutional structures. As coaches, we need to adapt and help others to keep learning – and to understand how people's sense of identity may change as technology continues to influence their lives.

This is the time when people most need to work together and develop a globally shared view of how technology is shaping our lives. As coaches, we need to help our leaders move away from traditional linear thinking and rise above their daily crises, to think strategically about how to innovate and manage disruption. As always, it comes down to people and values. We need to put people first and empower them if we want to avoid becoming de-humanised. While continuing to create and innovate, we need to maintain our compassion, empathy and stewardship, helping to forge a new collective sense of moral consciousness. This is where your roles as an organisational consultant, an individual coach and a team coach will be critical.

Should individual coaches and team coaches be trained differently?

Training and development matters profoundly, so leaders and coaches may have to be trained in very similar ways. It is essential for coaches to embrace technological change and be willing to alter the ways in which they see and manage their role as well as be flexible, in their interaction with clients. Coaches must continue to help clients harness critical thinking skills and develop their own capacity for change, skilfully guiding leaders to the limits of innovation – while transforming their own limiting assumptions underpinning their thinking and behaviour. The aim is to equip the leader to engage the best available thinking and innovative skills of their teams. Coaches need to help leaders focus on the experiences of systems wider than their organisation, opening themselves up to new ideas and perceptions. Coaches and leaders will be required to transform themselves. Changes to our educational curricula for leaders and coaches will have to evolve in order to stimulate and support such a dynamic transformation.

Thus, you need to think about your own continuing education and training as a thought leader. It is essential to constantly learn new models and processes to enhance your own coaching skills, and be persistent in developing your expertise in human and organisational systems, understanding how they function and change. This is the only way to absorb the thinking, feeling, attitudes, thinking patterns and behaviours that impact on team and organisational performance. And most importantly, it is necessary to constantly move away from being the expert while always developing your expertise.

Will the current coaching model still be applicable and good enough?

To achieve all these goals, in this digital era of transformation, we need to develop new and more innovative coaching models to suit our human systems. Our coaching will have to help leaders understand and manage power, conflict, leadership and systems (economic, technological and human). We live and work in a complex web of systems (families, societal groups, organisations, communities and nations) and our coaching models will have to support and encourage clients to navigate all this, recognising the matrix of systems of which they are a part. Executive and team coaching models need to help clients see past the role they occupy at any given moment.

What would you advise a new leader?

First is the importance of meeting with each member of staff, learning about them personally and professionally and fully understanding their roles and responsibilities. Equally important is being open to new ideas and thinking, letting every individual in your team know exactly what you as a leader are looking for and what you bring. A very effective way to achieve this is to run an open forum or small team coaching-type sessions to hear from everyone. We have a template of questions that we typically ask in a varied way with leaders as we start to work within their organisations. Sometimes, we work within a small team coaching session, or else in interviews with individual leaders. Questions to ask are as follows:

- What is working well, and what is not working well, within the organisation?
- Where do they want to be as an organisation, and what is preventing them from being where they want to be?

- How would they define their values and culture?
- How effective is the leadership team, and what needs to work better?
- How do the staff experience leadership, and what more do they need from their leaders and managers?
- What is holding everyone back in terms of thinking, feeling, attitudes, behaviour and performance?
- What values is the organisation working with, and what are the behaviours that give meaning to those values?
- What does the marketplace think of the organisation?
- What would aid your reputation in the marketplace and society?

Distributed leadership

The central components of leadership today are that it is a process which involves influence, occurs within a group context, and involves goal attainment (Ardichvili and Manderscheid, 2008: 620). Historically, empirical studies have researched leadership with a focus on the behaviours and skills of the individual leader. However, there is a growing recognition that leadership development is complex, and that it includes interactions between the leader and their social and organisational environments, embracing a more systemic and collective framework (Dalakoura, 2010: 433–438).

Leadership is thus seen as an activity that is "distributed" across multiple leaders, rather than inherent in the role of one leader (Spillane, 2005: 145). The traditional "heroic leader" is typically associated with the leader who single-handedly guides their organisation to greatness. An antidote to this is the concept of "distributed leadership". It suggests that, instead of leadership being seen as the culmination of a leader's competence and knowledge, leadership "practice" comprises a series of interactions between leaders, followers and their situation. In distributed leadership, although the emphasis is on leadership practice rather than on leadership roles, it does not necessarily imply an absence of hierarchy (Heikka, Waniganayake and Hujala, 2012: 34).

Originating with Senge's (1996) research into the learning organisation, distributed leadership emerged as a perspective on leadership "practice" rather than a "blueprint for effective leadership". It is not necessarily synonymous with shared leadership, team leadership or democratic leadership (Spillane, 2005: 149). According to Harris (2013), the two main concepts in distributed leadership are task distribution and the diffusion of influence as social interaction.

Other forms of leadership such as shared, collaborative or extended leadership practice are often confused with distributed leadership (Harris, 2013). Democratic leadership, which is associated with models of shared leadership, differs from distributed leadership where managerial tasks and responsibilities are redistributed, but not power and agency (Blackmore, 2006: 194). The value of distributed leadership and its usefulness to team coaches are as follows:

- the ability to look through a systemic lens at leadership activity;
- the potential for more democratic leadership;
- the possibility of greater efficiency and effectiveness as leadership activity and expertise are not "concentrated in one person" and
- that leaders will learn more about themselves and the critical issues facing their organisation (Mayrowetz, 2008: 425–431).

What's the difference between high performance and high potential?

The high performer is a key individual who contributes to the organisation's success and who demonstrates a high level of execution in their current role. A high-potential leader is an individual who has the ability, potential and aspiration for leadership positions within an organisation. They have a natural ability in higher level tasks. High-performance employees are very good at their jobs, whereas high-potential employees have demonstrated measurable skills and abilities beyond their current jobs. The real damage is done when the high-performance employee is promoted to a managerial level, is uncomfortable and struggles in their new role, resulting in high levels of stress and anxiety causing them to quit (Lombardo and Eichinger, 2000). According to Lombardo and Eichinger, learning from experience is how a person demonstrates what is termed high potential. Coaching, and particularly team coaching, is learning how to learn, and specifically learning from their own experience – with the ability to adapt with agility.

Learning agility for leadership teams

The essential components of Bill Joiner and Stephen Josephs' (2007) Agility Model are the potential to learn, the motivation to learn and the adaptability to learn. To become agile learners, we need to change the lens through which we view situations. Learning agility is a core leadership and team competence. It embraces the ability and willingness to learn from experience, subsequently applying that learning to perform under new or first-time conditions. "The signature skill of leaders is the ability to process new experiences … and to integrate them into their life" (Bennis and Thomas, 2002: 18). Leaders who are learning-agile are competent critical thinkers; they know themselves, can deal with the discomfort of change and can deliver results in new situations (De Meuse, Dai and Hallenbeck, 2009).

De Meuse, Dai, Hallenbeck and Tang (2008) claim that learning agility moves a high performer to a high-potential leader as they quickly develop the capacity for the following:

- *Self-awareness*: which includes the perception of oneself both in terms of strengths and in improving areas. Awareness can be effectively used in order to carry out one's role.
- *Mental agility*: which means facing complexity through curiosity as well as the capability to find an unusual, unique viewpoint in problems, in order to connect and find solutions in an innovative way.
- *People agility*: which requires openness towards others and relational flexibility so that differences do not represent obstacles but rather opportunities to be able to achieve objectives.
- *Change agility*: is agility that considers change as an opportunity to try new options and solutions, leading towards organisational changes.
- *Results agility*: is being motivated when facing challenges as well as developing the capacity to produce solutions in new situations, thus inspiring other people's actions (De Meuse et al., 2008).

Two core questions guided Joiner and Josephs' research into the agile leader: "What is it, exactly, that changes as a person grows from stage to stage, and how do leaders become more effective as they grow into more advanced stages?" (Joiner and Josephs, 2007: ix). The authors learned from their research that

> As you grow from one stage to another, you develop a distinct set of mental and emotional capacities that enable you to respond more effectively to change and complexity. In other words, leaders become more effective as they grow into the more advanced stages, because, in doing so, they become increasingly adept at responding to the degree of change and complexity that pervades today's workplace. In sum, the research shows that, as leaders move from one stage to another, their level of *leadership agility* increases.
>
> (Joiner and Josephs, 2007: ix–x)

Joiner and Josephs identified the following five developmental levels in mastering leadership agility:

- *Expert*: More of a supervisor than manager. Creates a group of individuals rather than a team. Works with direct reports primarily one-on-one. Too caught up in the details of their own work to lead in a strategic manner.
- *Achiever*: Operates like a full-fledged manager. Meetings to discuss important strategic or organisational issues are often orchestrated to try to gain buy-in to their own views.
- *Catalyst*: Intent on creating a highly participative team. Acts as a team leader and facilitator. Provides and seeks open exchange of views on difficult issues. Empowers direct reports. Uses team development as a vehicle for leadership development.
- *Co-Creator*: Develops a collaborative leadership team, where members feel full responsibility, not only for their own areas but also for the unit or organisation they collectively manage. Practical preference is for consensus decision-making, but they don't hesitate to use authority as needed.
- *Synergist*: Capable of moving fluidly between various team leadership styles uniquely suited to the situation at hand. Can shape or amplify the energy dynamics at work in a particular situation to bring about mutually beneficial results (Joiner and Josephs, 2007: 8–9).

These levels represent sets of emotional and mental capacities. As leaders advance through these levels, they are able to respond more effectively to change and complexity (Joiner and Josephs, 2007: ix–x). Heroic levels are those of the *Expert* and *Achiever*. At this level, managers assume *sole* responsibility for setting their organisation's objectives, coordinating the activities of their subordinates and managing their performance (Joiner and Josephs, 2007: 7). Post-heroic levels are identified as those of *Catalyst, Co-creator* and *Synergist*. Post-heroic leaders retain the "ultimate accountability and authority that comes with any formal leadership role. They work to create highly participative teams and organisations characterised by shared commitment and responsibility" (Joiner and Josephs, 2007: 10). According to their research, only 10 per cent of leaders today function at post-heroic levels of leadership.

This is important to us as team coaches because the leader's enhancement of their mental and emotional competence has a huge impact on their ability to develop the leadership agility of their own team members. These five levels of agility do not refer to personality types. In fact, no matter what the personality type, each leader has the potential to master advanced levels of agility (Joiner and Josephs, 2007: 12).

Teams versus work groups

Routine work is no longer predictable, nor are working conditions stable. "We now see a workforce that is moving quickly towards non-routine knowledge-based occupations and roles, which allow for much greater flexibility in terms of occupational roles, functions, hours, locations and working conditions" (Abrahamson, 2016: 5). This has significantly impacted how work is structured. No employee or leader can have the answers to all the questions and issues which arise daily within the operational complexity of business.

For this reason, organisations have integrated team-based structures into their daily organisational routine. Although "team" and "group" are often mentioned simultaneously, they differ in terms of their interdependence. A work group has a clearly focused leadership, and the group's purpose is the same as the broader organisational mission. However, members are part of the group only when together. The group is task focused, has individual work products and measures its effectiveness indirectly (Hawkins, 2014: 34).

A team, on the other hand, has shared leadership roles, and the team purpose can be different from the organisational mission. Work products are collective, generative dialogue is created with open discussion and active problem solving, members still act as part of the team when not together, and the team is task, process and learning focused. Performance is measured directly by assessing collective work products (Hawkins, 2014: 34).

Teams differ from groups primarily because they have a

> joint endeavour that they cannot achieve working either individually or in parallel … teams have a clear sense of shared purpose and interdependence on other members … and as teams rely on individual and collective accountability, team performance is higher as they produce outcomes based upon individual efforts and the joint contribution of their members: A team is more than the sum of its parts.
>
> (Carter and Hawkins, 2013: 178)

Team coaching versus facilitation

Clutterbuck (2007) and Hawkins (2011; 2014) have written some of the more comprehensive team coaching books that are informed by team effectiveness research. Clutterbuck (2007) recommends interventions that "improve performance when aimed at specific team processes or objectives", and Hawkins (2011; 2014) points out that team coaching has been loosely defined and used as an umbrella term that includes facilitation, team building and other group process interventions (Carr and Peters, 2013: 80).

Within most organisations, there is some confusion between "team coaching" and "group facilitation". It is important for anyone coaching teams or groups to be skilled not just in facilitating group learning processes but also in enabling coaching skills and competences for individual team members who need to develop their own direct reports in a coaching manner. Within an organisation, facilitation is most often used when people come together to work in teams. This style of management has become more prevalent in organisations today; hence, many team coaches require skills as facilitators.

In essence, the role of the team coach is to let the group become responsible for its aims and outcomes, and as the team coach to manage that group process. Hawkins describes team interventions as forming a continuum that moves from low internal complexity to high external complexity:

- *Team facilitation* (process focus).
- *Team performance coaching* (task and process focus).
- *Leadership team coaching* (task process and stakeholder focus).
- *Transformational leadership team coaching* (task, process, stakeholder and organisational transformation focus).
- *Systemic team coaching* (task, process, stakeholder, organisation and systems focus) (Hawkins, 2011: 62).

Team coaching is helpful in boosting the cohesion and effectiveness of functional teams within organisations. However, any leadership or management development strategy which includes individual and/or team coaching needs to be aligned with the client organisation's performance and business strategy. This includes the required behaviours, values, capabilities and competences which have been identified for a wide range of leadership and management roles. Often an organisation will be redefining their leadership brand through a comprehensive range of leadership development programmes implemented and measured over a one- to three-year period, complemented by an extensive individual, executive coaching intervention.

One of the main reasons for this is that leaders and managers need to be enabled to better facilitate quality conversations one-on-one with their direct reports, in team meetings and with stakeholders and customers. Often, prior to implementing a *leadership development programme*, a client organisation will already have identified the sets of behaviours which will help to create a results focus and performance orientation. The *individual coaching interventions* can be introduced with a range of *assessment profiles* to help with goal setting and leadership development planning, aligned to a *team coaching intervention* which may include those executives taking part in individual coaching interventions. This three-tier approach can address the emergent needs of management within an organisation, but at every stage visible behaviour change and performance need to be measured.

Other definitions of team coaching

The Centre for Conscious Leadership (CCL) describes team coaching as involving work with existing teams and project teams created for action learning purposes, and aimed at having an impact on the individual, team and organisational development. Team coaching may take the part of coaching an intact team, or a team which is a group of individuals brought together from across the organisation to accomplish a specific goal. CCL recommends conducting a thorough needs assessment to determine *team readiness* prior to any team coaching intervention (Ting and Scisco, 2006: 381–382, 400–401).

David Clutterbuck (2014: 271) defines team coaching as "a learning intervention designed to increase collective capability and performance of a group or team, through application of the coaching principles of assisted reflection, analysis and motivation for change". He describes the goals of team coaching as reliant on the stage of team development and the specific characteristics of the team. Clutterbuck (2014: 277) describes team coaching as often confused with team leading, team building, team facilitation and group therapy. Although there are overlaps, team coaching emphasises collective goals and action within the team.

He explains that to coach a team requires the same skills as to coach an individual – but to use them differently. I would say that a wider array of skills are needed to coach teams, particularly team facilitation skills, understanding how to manage team conflict, how to "sit in the fire without catching on fire" and being able to help the team emerge new thinking without being directive. Clutterbuck (2007) does say, however, that if you expect conflict, guide the team away from discord and towards productive interaction by reviewing its goals, motivations, values and methods. And accentuate shared achievements to raise their emotional intelligence, boost confidence and nurture their ability to handle stress.

Hawkins and Smith defined team coaching as "Enabling a team to function as more than the sum of its parts, by clarifying its mission and improving its external and internal relationships" (Hawkins and Smith, 2006: 62, quoted in Carter and Hawkins, 2013: 182). Hawkins further defined *Systemic Team Coaching*

> as a process by which a team coach works with a whole team, when they are together and when they are apart, in order to help them improve both their collective performance and how they work together, and also how they develop their collective leadership to engage more effectively with all their key stakeholder groups to jointly transform the wider business.
>
> (Carter and Hawkins, 2013: 182)

It has been argued that the Hackman and Wageman's (2005) definition of team coaching is generally used to represent the majority of team approaches in practice (O'Connor and Cavanagh, 2017: 496–497). However, O'Connor and Cavanagh express a cautionary note that there are five considerations for behavioural-based coaching which emerged from their qualitative research interviews:

1 *Outcomes of coaching*: including multiple potential goal levels of personal, interpersonal, team and organisational.
2 *The coach's approach*: identifying directive task-oriented versus relational process-oriented approaches.
3 *Timing of interventions*: referring to the interventions that tend to be used during the start, middle and end phases of a coaching engagement.
4 *Roles enacted though behaviour*: the four roles enacted by team coaches over an engagement were Advisory, Educational, Catalytic and Transitional.
5 *Influence on the coach's approach*: including personal attributes, background and experiences (O'Connor and Cavanagh, 2017: 496–497).

Clutterbuck's competences and five pillars for team coaching

David Clutterbuck explains that teams provide the bridge between individuals and the organisation, and that teams provide a sense of common identity, rooted in shared ideas, purpose, stories and attitudes, and an opportunity for conversation, support, recognition and other activities that make people feel motivated and raise self-esteem (Clutterbuck, 2007). He clarifies that individual coaching on its own will not necessarily create collective change: "coaching an individual without attempting to influence the immediate human systems in which they operate reduces the impact of the coaching intervention" (Clutterbuck, 2014: 272).

As advocated in the Kline Thinking Environment® model, "Addressing and improving the quality of thinking, for both individual issues and more broadly, is the core of coaching and this applies equally to individuals and the collective work group" (Clutterbuck, 2014: 272). However, he acknowledges that "there is an urgent need for empirical research to determine the roles and boundaries of team coaching" (Clutterbuck, 2014: 282).

Clutterbuck also suggests that in "the early stages of team formation, team coaching should be focused on clarifying the team task, setting norms of how to work together, defining boundaries and roles and gaining motivational momentum" (Clutterbuck, 2014: 273), but that a focus on "interpersonal relations (the core of team building) does not reliably improve team performance", and that team coaching is more effective if focused on motivation (Clutterbuck, 2014: 273).

Clutterbuck suggests that the most significant influences on a team's performance are diversity, conflict management and communication (Clutterbuck, 2014: 276), while the possible barriers to achieve their performance potential are a tendency towards social loafing, poor prioritisation of goals, failings in leadership and collective self-limiting beliefs (Clutterbuck, 2014: 279).

Clutterbuck has identified the following major team types to enable the team coach to become aware of the interpersonal dynamics within the team:

- *stable teams* (membership and tasks are constant);
- *cabin crew teams* (task remains the same, team changes constantly);
- *standing project teams* (stable new team created from a mix of other teams working on short-term projects);
- *evolutionary teams* (longer term projects with tasks and membership changing) and
- *developmental alliances* (teams set up for a learning objective) (Clutterbuck, 2014: 273).

Most importantly, Clutterbuck has identified the following core competences needed to be an effective team coach, which are in addition to the skills required to be an individual coach:

- managing varying paces of learning;
- managing sub-groups;
- maintaining confidentiality and
- facilitation (Clutterbuck, 2013: 1).

In addition, the following skills required for individual coaching are also demanded in team coaching but at a higher level:

- listening both to the person talking and to everyone else in the room;
- using silence effectively;
- asking powerful questions;
- helping a team to articulate its team identity and
- managing conflict (Clutterbuck, 2013: 1).

Clutterbuck's Team Coaching Certificate programme delivered by the School of Coaching (SCOA) in Milan, Italy, uses the CNIIC model as a template for enquiry and to structure the team coaching intervention. CNIIC stands for

- *Context* – the influence of the environment the team operates in;
- *Narrative* – the story the team tells itself and others about itself;
- *Identity* – the assumptions the team makes about how it should work and how;
- *Individual performance* – how each person chooses to work within the team and
- *Collective performance* – how the team combines the strength and energies of the team members to produce an optimum result (SCOA, 2018: 3).

Systemic team coaching

Modern approaches to organisational development and coaching practice tend to be based on the foundations of general systems theory as applied to human organisations and behaviour (Kilburg, 2000: 21). The emphasis is often on organisational diagnosis, process consultation, structural changes within teams and organisation, team facilitation, team building and individual and/or team coaching. Within organisations, human process interventions tend to focus on individuals, teams and groups.

Once you begin to work with an individual executive, their team often comes to the fore within a few sessions. Gaps within the team are identified in terms of decision-making, communication skills and facilitating or chairing meetings. Team coaching, which may be the next step, is becoming more affordable than individual executive coaching, and often ensures that the team is working together in alignment with organisational values and goals.

As a business coach, whether working with individuals or teams, you are helping your clients to learn from and interpret their own experiences, and to understand the complexity of the environment in which they work. *Systemic Team Coaching is essentially about the results experienced through the relationship between the coach, the individuals in the team, the resulting team dynamic, the organisational culture and the wider system within which the organisation works.*

Many organisations are not evolving innovative collective leadership processes, as they are working with outdated business management concepts and practices to deal with complex, multi-disciplinary issues. Teams are often hindered by interpersonal, disciplinary and organisational culture issues that prevent them from looking for new and better solutions.

Hawkins (2018a: 4–5) argues that

> A team's performance can best be understood through its ongoing ability to facilitate the creation of added value for the organisation it is part of, the organisation's investors, the team's internal and external customers and suppliers, its team members, the communities the team operates within and the more than human world in which we reside…as 'teamlanders' we can flourish only if we have a systemic perspective, an attitude of careful responsiveness and an ethic of collaboration.

Hawkins (2018b: 10) explains that to understand Systemic Team Coaching requires personal change at deeper levels of engagement, which he and Nick Smith define as data/definition of team, leadership and systemic coaching; behaviours; emotional ground (i.e. how to be and engage systemically); and underlying assumptions, beliefs and motivations (i.e. to be able to unlearn and relearn) (Hawkins and Smith, 2014).

Hawkins (2014: 107) defines Systemic Team Coaching as

> … a process by which a team coach works with a whole team, both when they are together and when they are apart, in order to help them improve both their collective performance and how they

work together, and also how they develop their collective leadership to more effectively engage with all their key stakeholder groups to jointly transform the wider business.

Leaders often set goals within their leadership teams, but have trouble communicating or supporting those objectives within the wider organisational system. To guarantee core learning, the coach helps the team learn as a collective while avoiding pitfalls such as working by trial and error, focusing obsessively on the past, emphasising theory or analysis without action or expecting the organisation to execute the team's plans without change or comment.

Conclusion

The dizzying challenges from digital technology and artificial intelligence, driven by the Fourth Industrial Revolution, impact on how we define team coaching, learning facilitation and leadership development. In today's race to digitalise, we need to grasp the importance of leadership agility and the difference between a high-potential employee and a high-potential leader. In Chapter 4, we explore a variety of leadership team coaching models, including the ones which have most influenced the development and working of my team coaching process. In the following chapter, Deborah Williams shares her experience in transforming leaders and organisational culture through a transformational leadership coaching programme.

References

Abrahamson, D. (2016). *Team Coaching: Why, Where, When and How.* WABC White Paper, Best Fit Business Coaching Series. Saanichton, BC: WABC Coaches.

Ardichvili, A., and Manderscheid, S.V. (2008). Emerging practices in leadership development. *Advances in Developing Human Resources*, 10(5):619–631.

Bennis, W.G., and Thomas, R.J. (2002). *Geeks and Geezers: How Era, Values and Defining Moments Shape Leaders.* Boston, MA: Harvard Business School Press.

Blackmore, J. (2006). Social justice and the study and practice of leadership in education: A feminist history. *Journal of Educational Administration and History*, 38(2):185–200.

Carr, C., and Peters, J. (2013). The experience of team coaching: A dual case study. *International Coaching Psychology Review*, 8(1):80–98.

Carter, A., and Hawkins, P. (2013). Team coaching. In Passmore, J., Peterson, D.B., and Freire, T. (eds), *The Wiley-Blackwell Handbook of the Psychology of Coaching and Mentoring*, pp. 175–194. Oxford: Wiley.

Clutterbuck, D. (2007). *Coaching the Team at Work.* London: Nicholas Brealey.

Clutterbuck, D. (2013). *The Competencies of an Effective Team Coach*. URL: www.davidclutterbuckpartnership.com/the-competencies-of-an-effective-team-coach/. Accessed 14 May 2018.

Clutterbuck, D. (2014). Team coaching. In Cox, E., Bachkirova, T., and Clutterbuck, D. (eds), *The Complete Handbook of Coaching*, pp. 271–284. Second Edition. London: Sage.

Dalakoura, A. (2010). Differentiating leader and leadership development: A collective framework for leadership development. *Journal of Management Development*, 29(5):432–441.

De Meuse, K.P., Dai, G., and Hallenbeck, G.S. (2009). *The Many Faces of Learning Agility: An Excerpt from the 2010 Mid-Winter Conference of Consulting Psychology in Scottsdale, AZ*. PowerPoint presentation. Los Angeles, CA: Korn/Ferry International.

De Meuse, K.P., Dai, G. Hallenbeck, G.S., and Tang, K.Y. (2008). *Using Learning Agility to Identify High Potentials around the World*. Research study. Los Angeles, CA: Korn Ferry Institute.

Hackman, J.R., and Wageman, R. (2005). A theory of team coaching. *Academy of Management Review*, 30:269–287.

Harris, A. (2013). Distributed leadership: Friend or foe? *Educational Management Administration and Leadership*, 41(5):545–554.

Hawkins, P. (2011). *Leadership Team Coaching: Developing Collective Transformational Leadership*. London: Kogan Page.

Hawkins, P. (2014). *Leadership Team Coaching: Developing Collective Transformational Leadership*. Second Edition. London: Kogan Page.

Hawkins, P. (2018a). Introduction: Highly effective teams – the latest research and development. In Hawkins, P. (ed.), *Leadership Team Coaching in Practice: Developing High-Performing Teams*, pp. 1–8. Second Edition. London: Kogan Page.

Hawkins, P. (2018b). What are leadership team coaching and systemic team coaching? In Hawkins, P. (ed.), *Leadership Team Coaching in Practice: Developing High-Performing Teams*, pp. 9–22. Second Edition. London: Kogan Page.

Hawkins, P., and Smith, N. (2006). *Coaching, Mentoring and Organisational Consultancy: Supervision and Development*. Maidenhead: Open University Press/McGraw Hill.

Hawkins, P., and Smith, N. (2014). Transformational coaching. In Cox, E., Bachkirova, T., and Clutterbuck, D. (eds), *The Complete Handbook of Coaching*, pp. 228–243. Second Edition. London: Sage.

Heikka, J., Waniganayake, M., and Hujala, E. (2012). Contextualising distributed leadership within early childhood education: Current understandings, research evidence and future challenges. *Educational Management Administration and Leadership*, 41(1):30–44.

Joiner, B., and Josephs, S. (2007). *Leadership Agility: Five Levels of Mastery for Anticipating and Initiating Change*. San Francisco, CA: Jossey-Bass.

Kilburg, R.R. (2000). *Executive Coaching: Developing Managerial Wisdom in a World of Chaos*. Washington, DC: American Psychological Association.

Lombardo, M.M., and Eichinger, R.W. (2000). High-potentials as high learners. *Human Resource Management*, 39(4):321–330.

Mayrowetz, D. (2008). Making sense of distributed leadership: Exploring the multiple usages of the concept in the field. *Educational Administration Quarterly*, 44(3):424–435.

O'Connor, S., and Cavanagh, M. (2017). Group and team coaching. In Bachkirova, T., Spence, G., and Drake, D. (eds), *The Sage Handbook of Coaching*, pp. 488–506. London: Sage.

School of Coaching (SCOA). (2018). *Team Coaching Certificate*. Milan: SCOA.

Senge, P.M. (1996). Leading learning organisations: The bold, the powerful, and the invisible. In Hesselbein, R., Goldsmith, M., and Beckhard, R. (eds), *The Leader of the Future: New Visions, Strategies, and Practices for the Next Era*, pp. 41–48. San Francisco, CA: Jossey-Bass.

Spillane, J.P. (2005). Distributed leadership. *The Educational Forum*, 69(2):143–150.

Susskind, R., and Susskind, D. (2015). *The Future of the Professions: How Technology Will Transform the Work of Human Experts*. Oxford: Oxford University Press.

Ting, S., and Scisco, P. (eds) (2006). *The CCL Handbook of Coaching: A Guide for the Leader Coach*. San Francisco, CA: Jossey-Bass.

3 Transformative leadership coaching

Shifting culture in organisations

Deborah Williams

Most organisations face the challenge of empowering leaders to lead effectively while fostering an enabling team culture throughout the organisation. An enabling culture is one that encourages high engagement and performance from employees – to facilitate outperformance in the delivery of organisational objectives, with the aim of delivering strategy and purpose.

Coaching has emerged as one of the most effective tools for transforming leadership and organisational culture. Coaching motivates leaders to lead authentically – interacting positively in relationships and building a culture in which their teams can flourish. Coaching empowers leaders to integrate effectively within the broader organisational system, helping them understand the web of relationships and the complexity of the organisation and its external stakeholders. Systemic Team Coaching and individual coaching both result in the personal transformation of the leader, challenging leaders to focus on growing their teams while working in a matrix organisation and improving relationships with stakeholders and customers (Williams, 2017).

This chapter explores reflections and insights on leadership development, coaching and organisational culture and their impact on increasing business performance. It includes a case study of a division of 3,000 employees within a large financial services company, from my perspective as an Organisational Development consultant in a human capital department. Late in 2015, the Division restructured six smaller businesses with diverse sub-cultures in three main regional offices, into one Business Unit under a Chief Executive Officer (CEO) and an Executive Team. The merger meant extensive change, which required leaders to continually adapt to a complex environment – at the same time ensuring that their teams delivered optimally to customers and stakeholders. In August 2016, the Division redefined its client-operating model and split the Division into three different legal entities to service the different client divisions. This led to restructuring, retrenchments and the announcement of new organisational structures to ensure the realisation of the business's value proposition.

The Transformative Leadership Coaching Programme integrated Systemic Team Coaching and individual coaching. It was an Organisational Development project which I introduced to empower executive and senior leaders in one of the largest business units in the Division. The first step was to gain approval from the CEO and the Divisional Human Capital Executive to implement the programme. We also required the full involvement of the General Manager for the Business Unit, as she was the Executive Manager of the 19 senior leaders who were to participate in the programme. In April 2016, I initiated a partnership between myself as the Organisational Development consultant and Sunny Stout-Rostron to deliver Systemic Team Coaching over a 12-month period. In addition, we arranged that each leader would receive monthly individual coaching sessions. The coaching was provided by Sunny as lead coach, plus two external coaches and myself as an internal coach to work with Team B.

The key aim of the coaching programme was to develop in these leaders the leadership behaviours required to lead self, teams and the organisation to achieve the organisation's strategic goals. The objectives were for the CEO and the Divisional Human Capital Executive to

- support leaders in developing personal insight and transforming self;
- support leaders in developing an outward mind-set and the leadership behaviours aligned to the organisation's culture;
- provide personal support to leaders in their roles and to impact their levels of motivation and overall physical and emotional wellbeing;
- support leaders in effectively leading their teams to excel in the organisational environment;
- support leaders in developing their ability to communicate and influence peers, internal stakeholders and external stakeholders and
- support leaders to lead and manage change.

The programme design for this coaching programme was to develop transformative leadership that would build an organisational culture promoting team performance.

Strategy's link to organisational leadership and culture

Leadership, culture and organisational performance are integrally linked and are essential for the attainment of an organisation's strategy. Organisational culture can be described as the shared values, beliefs or perceptions held by employees within an organisation or organisational unit (Robbins and Coulter, 2005). Culture is seen as the organisation's way of perceiving and doing things. Schein (2004: 17) defined the culture of a group or organisation as a

> pattern of shared basic assumptions that was learned by a group as it solved its problems of external adaptation and internal integration, that has worked well enough to be considered valid and, therefore, to be taught to new members as the correct way to perceive, think, and feel in relation to those problems.

Organisational culture

Empirical research has provided impressive evidence on the role of organisational culture in improving performance (Denison and Mishra, 1995). The most important aspect of Schein's (2004) definition is that it is based on shared assumptions, thoughts and feelings of the group, and these determine much of the behaviour and norms of how things are done (or not done) in the organisation. In this way, culture has a direct impact on organisational performance. The culture manifests itself through the underlying assumptions and is seen in the processes, the physical environment, organisational structures and organisational engagement processes. The shared beliefs and values include the organisation's philosophy, mission, goals and strategy (Schein, 2004).

The Executive Committee (ExCo) of the newly merged Division prioritised cultural change together with other strategic business goals. They reviewed the current culture of the Division and outlined an *enabling culture* that would support the achievement of strategic goals. Each executive leader embarked on a coaching process, spearheaded by the Divisional Human Capital Executive, to understand the current culture in their areas, and to work towards transforming their own leadership behaviour, positively influencing the culture of their teams. This was not, however, sufficient – leaders at a senior manager level also needed to be transformed.

In a key document, the organisation had outlined the values and behaviours expected of employees. All leaders participated in workshops to understand this. In my experience, workshops or training are not sufficient to change the behaviour of a leader. In February 2016, an Organisational Human Factor Benchmarking Survey designed by Afriforte (2016) was conducted in the Business Unit in which the leaders were participating in the Transformative Leadership Coaching Programme. The purpose of the survey was to benchmark the organisational climate and understand the dynamics in the work environment.

The results suggested an unhealthy climate, indicating that employees would not be able to act on the strategic intent of the organisation. This survey provided the organisation with a baseline assessment of the current climate and some of the leadership, management, employee wellbeing, employee engagement and broader issues that leaders needed to focus on to build an enabling culture. The findings endorsed the need for an intervention at the senior level of leadership that would support transforming leadership and building an enabling culture.

Leadership and transforming an organisational culture require an ongoing and targeted intervention that influences change in how senior managers, managers and team leaders lead. Coaching offers a more sustainable opportunity for leadership and culture change. The Transformative Leadership Coaching Programme was identified as a critical programme towards the goal and was fully endorsed by the ExCo.

A greater necessity for the Transformative Leadership Coaching Programme emerged halfway into the project – after the integration of the six businesses into one unit. The redesign of the operating model had resulted in massive change, and in some cases, retrenchments. All the Systemic Team Coaching sessions and most of the individual coaching sessions provided a platform for leaders to reflect on the changes and to redefine their role as leaders.

Cultural diversity and organisational culture

In South Africa, cultural and gender transformation present a challenge as organisations attempt to identify black and women leaders for senior and executive leadership positions. A key element of an enabling culture is the integration of diversity into the organisational culture, and the consideration of diversity issues such as culture, age, sex, rank, gender and sexual orientation.

Transformation had been a key priority in the Business Unit where I worked, due to the unit's involvement with public sector clients in South Africa. This meant that 90 per cent of the senior leaders involved in the coaching programmes were Black, but only 10 per cent were female. The diversity in the organisation had allowed for the unique strengths of the different cultures to influence the conception of an enabling culture. Diversity has been entrenched within the company by making it one of the organisation's six core values, together with integrity, accountability, teamwork, excellence and innovation.

Transforming leadership

Leaders in organisations are currently being challenged to focus on the delivery of operational goals, as well as to inspire a team of diverse members. Mastering the art of leading as well as managing is not easy in an organisation when there are high operational demands and a focus on performance.

Leadership behaviour affects organisational culture, whereas culture impacts on the development of the leader (Avolio Howell and Avolio, 1993; Schein, 2004). Transactional leaders tend to operate within the limits of the existing culture, whereas transformational leaders contribute to changing the organisational culture in line with their vision for the potential of the organisation (Bass, 1985). Leaders need to first change their own behaviours to align with the envisaged or desired culture, before they can create an enabling culture in their teams. This requirement to lead by example necessitates that they become more conscious of their own behaviours and attitudes as they operate within the organisational system and interact with their teams.

As an organisation, we had identified leaders as being in the best position to influence a change in culture (Schein, 2004). Most leaders I was working with did not seem to realise that their own behaviour modelled or reinforced a particular culture. Transforming assumptions and beliefs to those of an enabling culture is one of the key responsibilities of leaders. It requires authentic leaders who are critically self-aware and constantly taking a deep look at how they think and behave, based on their values and moral perspectives (Avolio, Luthans and Walumbwa, 2004; Gatling, Castelli and Cole, 2013). Authentic leadership focuses on four competencies (Walumbwa, Avolio, Gardner, Wernsing and Peterson, 2008):

- self-awareness (of values, thoughts and emotions);
- relational transparency (ability to reveal thoughts, emotions and information to others);
- balanced treatment of information (openness to feedback) and
- internalised moral perspective when taking action (Walumbwa et al., 2008: 92).

The challenge was to implement a leadership coaching programme that would support leaders to go on their own journey of change and transform their way of leading at personal, team and organisational levels to have a positive impact on business results (Stout-Rostron, 2012). As an Organisational Development consultant, I knew that as more leaders transformed their leadership behaviour, the transformative capability in the organisation would grow and an enabling culture would emerge and be entrenched (Arnold and Prescher, 2017).

In my view, leadership development training programmes would not sufficiently address the challenge of shifting organisational culture while developing values-based leadership in the Division. Many studies have confirmed coaching as an effective leadership development tool (Peltier, 2010; Theeboom, Beersma and Van Vianen, 2013). An integration of Systemic Team Coaching and individual coaching appeared to be the best intervention to support leaders in demonstrating the organisational values in daily behaviour, encouraging their teams to live the values, actively aligning to the organisational purpose and achieving high levels of performance.

An integrated coaching framework to shift organisational culture

Business coaching, which includes individual and team coaching, provides highly focused and accelerated learning within the context of an organisation (Chapman and Cilliers, 2008). O'Neill (2000) provided a stronger link between coaching and organisational culture when she stated that the essence of coaching is "helping leaders work through their challenges, so they can transform their learning into results for the organisation" (O'Neill, 2000: 5). A coaching programme should offer leaders an opportunity to consider the business realities they face and develop appropriate skills and behaviours as they grow in their self-awareness (Terblanche, Albertyn and Van Coller-Peter, 2017). It should also lead to improvements in the leadership and management practices of leaders with their teams.

Systemic Team Coaching to align organisational culture, systems and relationships

Team coaching has taken longer to evolve as a leadership development and cultural change tool than individual coaching. The more traditional team coaching approaches focused on internal aspects of the growth of the team, and not sufficiently on external performance and supporting the development of an enabling culture throughout the organisation. Systemic Team Coaching facilitated by a team coach allows for leaders to learn together as a team to improve their collective performance and to develop their collective leadership more effectively (Hawkins, 2012: 78).

A key focus would be to engage with the underlying assumptions of the leaders, as well as how they view the cultural artefacts, including the systems, processes and structures in the newly merged environment (Schein, 2004). Systemic Team Coaching provides a platform for leaders to explore the espoused beliefs and values in the organisation and to develop a clearer understanding and commitment to the philosophy, goals and strategy of the organisation. In this way, Systemic Team Coaching contributes to leaders increasing their effectiveness in the organisation and contributing to an enabling organisational culture.

Individual coaching to entrench individual learning and leadership change

Coaching contributes to leaders' personal growth, allowing them to change at a deeper level, and increases their effectiveness in relationships with people and in the organisation (Karsten, 2010). Individual business, or executive coaching, complements Systemic Team Coaching and strengthens the capability of leaders to lead effectively in their particular context. Individual coaching is based on a confidential relationship with a professional coach. In this one-on-one coaching relationship, a leader can overcome a sense of vulnerability in the face of complex challenges as they explore issues they are facing on an individual and organisational level (Reynolds, 2011; Williams, 2017). This allows for deep reflection in which leaders are able to grow in self-awareness, as they deepen understanding of their thoughts and feelings, learn from their mistakes and improve their leadership effectiveness (Cox, 2006). Coaching provides leaders with permanent transformative learning in one or more of their visible behaviours, which, in turn, affects the behaviour and performance of those in their teams (Rekalde, Landeta, and Albizu, 2015).

The rest of this chapter tells the story of some of the interesting "learnings" from the Transformative Leadership Coaching Programme that we implemented in our organisation through a close working relationship between myself as the internal Organisational Development consultant and coach, and an external coach, Sunny Stout-Rostron, an expert in relational and organisational coaching. It also reports on the findings of a research study that I conducted in 2017 at the end of the programme.

Coaching within an organisational system

I was conscious of my responsibility to ensure that the coaching programme introduced into the organisation added business value to internal stakeholders by contributing to leadership effectiveness and a new enabling culture. At the same time, it needed to create value by meeting the expectations of external stakeholders, including customers, investors and the community (Ulrich and Dulebohn, 2015).

Hawkins (2009) suggested that organisations require a meaningful coaching strategy grounded in the business strategy that is aligned to the wider organisational culture. I applied the four main pillars of this strategy to evaluate to what extent we applied best practice in the programmatic design and implementation and to derive learnings for introducing future coaching programmes.

1 Start with the end in mind

   The need for the coaching programme was first identified in a business project, adopted by ExCo to improve the performance of the Business Unit. The people stream of this project had recognised that transforming leadership was a critical need in the business. This was confirmed by the findings of the Organisational Human Factor Benchmarking Survey. The general manager of the Business Unit requested that the Organisational Development Department submit a proposal for a coaching intervention. The proposal submitted provided the business case for the coaching and outlined the organisational outcomes of the programme. The relevance of the programmatic design with a focus on transforming leadership and culture resulted in the business authorising the coaching programme, allocating funding to contract external coaching resources.

2 Design the right mix of internal and external resources

   I initiated the programme by contracting Sunny Stout-Rostron to design and provide the Systemic Team Coaching intervention which would complement the individual coaching. We agreed that, as the internal coach, I would assist in preparing and co-facilitating the sessions. This evolved into joint planning of the sessions. As the internal coach, I provided regular updates on organisational changes within the business and gave perspective in each team coaching session. The co-facilitation model provided internal integration with other organisational initiatives, thus ensuring higher levels of organisational impact.

The Society for Industrial and Organisational Psychology (SIOP, 2018) suggests that it is likely that external coaches are most effective when working with leaders at higher levels in the organisation, or when there is a culture of low trust. They see the use of internal coaches as a more viable and cost-effective option at the middle level of leadership. As an internal coach, I would be more accessible and able to provide continuity in the programme. I initially allocated the six executive leaders for individual coaching to Sunny Stout-Rostron due to her extensive executive coaching experience, planning to coach the other 13 senior leaders myself to save costs.

I soon realised that, due to time constraints, this was not feasible, and we subsequently contracted another two external coaches to join the coaching team. My dual role as Organisational Development consultant and internal coach presented several constraints and ethical dilemmas in relation to neutrality, confidentiality and conflicts of interest (Babbie and Mouton, 2001; SIOP, 2018). Honesty and boundary setting, as well as confidentiality, were pivotal in the contracting sessions (SIOP, 2018). One candidate felt I knew him too well and requested an external coach.

We ensured internal integration of the individual and team coaching intervention with other organisational initiatives, conducting two thorough business-briefing sessions with the external coaches. The first session provided an overview of the organisational vision and strategic goals, and provided the context for organisational change that had occurred as the result of the merger in our Division. In the second session, I requested that one of our industrial psychologists provide individual feedback to the coaches on each individual coachee, including their role, years in the business and a synopsis of their Cognitive Processing Profile assessment.

In our final programme review, we concluded that the model, including internal and external coaches on a large coaching programme, offered an effective integrated coaching programme to Team B. It provided tight parameters to protect the individuals being coached as well as the organisation.

3 Create a coaching culture

The business had not previously used coaching as a leadership intervention. According to Hawkins (2012: 21),

> A coaching culture exists in an organisation when a coaching approach is a key aspect of how the leaders, managers, and staff engage and develop all their people and engage their

stakeholders, in ways that create increased individual, team and organisational performance and shared value for all stakeholders.

The introduction of the integrated coaching programme laid the foundation for future programmes and for a coaching culture to emerge in the organisation.

Terblanche et al. (2017) suggested that, to ensure a successful coaching programme, mentors, line managers and the new leader's team must be involved in the coaching process. Unfortunately, this process of mentoring was not introduced to support the integrated coaching programme, and should be a key consideration for future initiatives.

All of our organisational consultants recently committed themselves to becoming accredited organisational relationship and systems team coaches, in order to sustain such interventions internally. I anticipate that, as more coaching programmes are introduced into different parts of the business and the organisation develops a coaching policy, a coaching culture will evolve.

4 Have a process to capture the organisational learning

This was captured in four ways. The first was through the joint reflective sessions held monthly between myself, as Organisational Development consultant, and Sunny Stout-Rostron. The second was through the reflections and writing of Sunny Stout-Rostron, where aspects of the learning have contributed to this book. The third was through coaching supervision. The fourth was through the research assignment I completed on the coaching intervention as part of my MPhil degree in Management Coaching. The intention was to present the findings of this research to the Human Capital Executive Team and the Business Unit ExCo for their input in relation to future interventions.

One of the ways to capture organisational learning was to put in place a coaching supervision process. Hawkins and Schwenk (2006, cited in Hawkins and Turner, 2017) defined coach supervision as a structured and formal process facilitated by a coaching supervisor to assist coaches in improving the quality of their coaching and in improving their coaching practice. Two sessions were held with all the coaches together. Further supervision was provided in one-on-one supervision sessions with Sunny Stout-Rostron as a lead coach and supervisor. Our learning has been to have had all of us, including the lead coach, supervised as a group by another external coach supervisor.

Reflections on implementing a Transformative Leadership Coaching Programme

At the end of the coaching intervention, I conducted a qualitative research study entitled "Exploration of Leaders' Experience of Transformative Learning through Coaching in the Financial Insurance Industry" to assess how the coaching had transformed leaders. The focus of the interviews was on the individual coaching, but many participants had both the individual coaching and Systemic Team Coaching in mind when they answered the questions, and some referred specifically to the team coaching in their discussions.

The research found that

> the process of transformative learning through the coaching contributed to personal transformation, helping leaders to develop personal insight, gain perspective on their thoughts and feelings and become more open and emotionally able to engage in change. Significant shifts were seen in the way in which leaders interacted with others, especially their teams, and improved their leadership and management practices. The findings confirm that the coaching equipped leaders to manage uncertainty and adapt to organisational change.
>
> (Williams, 2017: iv)

It was therefore clear that the coaching had contributed to a shift in leadership culture and organisational culture. Below are a few excerpts of evidence from the research study (Williams, 2017).

Many of the leaders in Team B shared that they had become conscious of how others experienced them as a leader. They reported a realisation that they were affecting others in a negative or non-developmental way through some of their behaviours and showed a positive commitment to build a more enabling culture in their teams:

> I've needed to reflect quite deeply about how I behaved in the past…I needed to reflect, critically self-reflect and say, 'What am I doing for people to not really be comfortable to talk to me about difficult issues? Am I too impatient? Am I too critical?'
>
> I didn't realise what I was doing to other people…I probably didn't even know. But the biggest insight is my execution and how I make people feel. I didn't know I was having such an impact. I had a seriously negative impact on people. Don't do that, man. Why?

Evidence of new thinking on what it means to be an enabling and authentic leader emerged from the interviews:

> The leader is not the one on the pedestal. The leader is the one behind the scenes, enabling. I guess that he enables the atmosphere, enables the vision…You always need to have your clear picture of where you need to go and why and all these things, but when it comes to people you need to be able to take them on the journey with you. Because it is ours.

All leaders reported a shift in their leadership behaviours and spoke of new behaviours in the way in which they socially interacted with their teams to foster an enabling culture:

> So, for me, the big conversations we had were about me and how I was managing my people. And that was the word, 'managing'. Because that's what I was doing – managing their time, managing their activities and not allowing them to grow and develop, and also not coaching, growing or developing them so they are able to help me lead.
>
> I think the coaching has helped me understand the power that you can pull out of people just by changing how you engage with them.

A few shared how, through the coaching, they had actively worked to build an enabling culture:

> It allowed me as an individual to start growing the ability to observe, to see, and systemically see things that are happening in the business from a behavioural perspective – both in terms of how leaders should behave and also how leaders should behave in line with our culture, values…

The research study (Williams, 2017) concluded with a strong business case for introducing coaching programmes to transform organisational culture. It confirmed that as leaders transform self, they develop a readiness to lead a values-based culture. It challenges the definition of business coaching and broadens it to suggest that it should "benefit not only personal growth in the leader, but also influence the leader to develop a more outward focus to support their teams, peers, internal and external stakeholders and customers to achieve overall business goals" (Williams, 2017: 61).

Conclusion

This chapter explored the reflections and insights gained after introducing a Transformative Leadership Coaching Programme into an organisation as an effective intervention for transforming leadership and culture and contributing to improved business performance. It provides a strong rationale for introducing both Systemic Team Coaching and individual coaching as an integrated coaching intervention. It provides some interesting perspectives and insights for Organisational Development consultants and human resource business partners to work in partnership with external coaches to collaboratively transform organisational culture through coaching.

References

Afriforte. (2016). *The Organisational Human Factor Benchmark*. URL: www.afriforte.com/home/the-organisational-human-factor-benchmark/. Accessed 5 March 2018.

Arnold, R., and Prescher, T. (2017). From transformative leadership to transformative learning: New approaches in leadership development. In Laros, A., Thomas, F., and Taylor, E.W. (eds), *Transformative Learning Meets Bildung: An International Exchange*, pp. 281–294. Rotterdam: Sense.

Avolio, B.J., Luthans, F., and Walumbwa, F.O. (2004). *Authentic Leadership: Theory Building for Veritable Sustained Performance*. Working Paper. Lincoln, NE: Gallup Leadership Institute, University of Nebraska-Lincoln.

Avolio Howell, J.M., and Avolio, B.J. (1993). Transformational leadership, transactional leadership, locus of control and support for innovation: Key predictors of consolidated-business-unit performance. *Journal of Applied Psychology*, 78:891–902.

Babbie, E.R., and Mouton, J. (2001). *The Practice of Social Research*. Cape Town: Oxford University Press Southern Africa.

Bass, B.M. (1985). *Leadership and Performance*. New York, NY: Free Press.

Chapman, L., and Cilliers, F. (2008). The integrated experiential executive coaching model: A qualitative exploration. *South African Journal of Labour Relations*, 32(1):63–80.

Cox, E. (2006). An adult learning approach to coaching. In Stober, D., and Grant, A.M. (eds), *Evidence-Based Coaching Handbook: Putting Best Practices to Work for Your Clients*, pp. 193–217. Hoboken, NJ: Wiley.

Denison, D., and Mishra, A. (1995). Towards a theory of organisational culture and effectiveness. *Organisation Science*, 6:204–223.

Gatling, A.R., Castelli, P.A., and Cole, M.L. (2013). Authentic leadership: The role of self-awareness in promoting coaching effectiveness. *Asia-Pacific Journal of Management Research and Innovation*, 9(4):337–347.

Hawkins, P. (2009). Developing an effective coaching strategy. *Global Focus: The EFMD Business Magazine*, Special supplement, 3(3):15–19.

Hawkins, P. (2012). *Creating a Coaching Culture.* Maidenhead: Open University Press.

Hawkins, P., and Schwenk, G. (2006). *Coaching Supervision: Maximising the Potential of Coaching.* London: CIPD.

Hawkins, P., and Turner, E. (2017). The rise of coaching supervision 2006 to 2014. *Coaching: An International Journal of Theory, Research and Practice,* 10(2):102–114.

Karsten, M. (2010). Coaching: An effective leadership intervention. *Nursing Clinics of North America*, 45(1):39–48.

O'Neill, M.B. (2000). *Executive Coaching with Backbone and Heart: A Systems Approach to Engaging Leaders with Their Challenges.* San Francisco, CA: Jossey-Bass.

Peltier, B. (2010). *The Psychology of Executive Coaching: Theory and Application.* Second Edition. New York, NY: Routledge.

Rekalde, I., Landeta, J., and Albizu, E. (2015). Determining factors in the effectiveness of executive coaching as a management development tool. *Management Decision*, 53(8):1677–1697.

Reynolds, G. (2011). Exploring the meaning of coaching for newly-appointed senior leaders in their first twelve to eighteen months in role. *International Journal of Evidence-Based Coaching and Mentoring*, Special Issue 5:39–53.

Robbins, S.P., and Coulter, M. (2005). *Management.* Eighth Edition. Upper Saddle River, NJ: Prentice Hall.

Schein, E.H. (2004). *Organisational Culture and Leadership.* Third Edition. San Francisco, CA: Jossey-Bass.

Society for Industrial and Organisational Psychology (SIOP). (2018). *Challenges Associated with Internal Coaching.* URL: www.siop.org/Workplace/coaching/internal_versus_exte.aspx. Accessed 10 March 2018.

Stout-Rostron, S. (2012). *Business Coaching Wisdom and Practice: Unlocking the Secrets of Business Coaching.* Second Edition. Johannesburg: Knowres.

Terblanche, N.H.D., Albertyn, R.M., and Van Coller-Peter, S. (2017). Designing a coaching intervention to support leaders promoted into senior positions. *SA Journal of Human Resource Management*, 15(0):a842. doi:10.4102/sajhrm.v15i0.842. Accessed 5 March 2018.

Theeboom, T., Beersma, B., and Van Vianen, A. (2013). Does coaching work? A meta-analysis on the effects of coaching on individual level outcomes in an organisational context. *The Journal of Positive Psychology*, 9(1):1–18.

Ulrich, D., and Dulebohn, J.H. (2015). Are we there yet? What's next for HR? *Human Resource Management Review*, 25(2):188–204.

Walumbwa, F.O., Avolio, B.J., Gardner, W.L., Wernsing, T.S., and Peterson, S.J. (2008). Authentic leadership: Development and validation of a theory-based measure. *Journal of Management*, 34(1):89–126.

Williams, D. (2017). *Exploration of Leaders' Experience of Transformative Learning through Coaching in the Financial Insurance Industry.* Unpublished M.Phil. dissertation. Bellville: University of Stellenbosch Business School.

4 Theories, models and tools informing the High-Performance Relationship Coaching Model

Sunny Stout-Rostron

Business issues today often call for a diverse set of knowledge, skill sets and innovative perspectives. This requires moving outside of the traditional view of teams and what they need to operate and be supported. Research demonstrates that successful teamwork needs appropriate team design and structure, team inauguration and ongoing team coaching facilitated by competent and well-trained team coaches. The foundation for improved performance also requires the creation of a "real" team with a compelling purpose, employing the right people, a solid structure, a supportive environment and team coaching at the right time (Abrahamson, 2016: 3).

Systems thinking and human relationship systems

To understand the structure and mechanics of building a team coaching model, I found it useful to study the basic concepts behind systems thinking. Models are systems. "A system is a concept constructed to solve a problem" (McWhinney, Webber, Smith and Novokowsky, 1996: 13), and a coaching model is *a construct to create the space that defines where the coach and the client work*. A system is about the relation of the parts to the whole.

Understanding systems and structure is vital to build a team coaching model. Systems thinking has become a popular approach to understand how organisations, business and people behave – and the concepts of organisation and wholeness are crucial to grasp how systems operate. When dealing with human systems, we are always concerned with the relationships between the people in the system – and that is where we work as team coaches.

The family is the immediate system with which we are all familiar. A shared field of interests defines a "family system". "Boundaries between the sub-systems are marked by the relation between the people within a family (enmeshed, closed, and separated)" (McWhinney, 1993: ii–iii). Family system therapies developed to explain individual behaviour "arising from the behaviour of the family system or of the immediate family plus other relevant people and institutions" (McWhinney, 1993: 45). Systems theory, although originally developed to work with the nuclear family, was seen to be very relevant to organisations, teams and other work groups and communities, that is, work, social, cultural and religious groups.

In coaching, we are particularly concerned with "human and organisational systems" and how they function and change. In the larger system, it is the others that the team members relate to, both in terms of covert and overt relationships which are internal and external to the organisation. Finally, human societies create systems of beliefs which become worldviews defining the culture that is created within an organisation. A leader's role is to help people see and understand each other's perspectives – in order to develop understanding, empathy and teamwork. That is one of your core roles as a team coach.

"Systems thinking" has its roots in engineering theories and cybernetics. Originally, it was concerned with self-regulating systems and feedback loops that maintained the system's stability. "Systems thinking" follows a circular logic; it looks at the whole rather than component parts of the whole. This idea of circularity has had a strong influence on my team coaching model, the High-Performance Relationship Coaching Model.

Teams A, B and C

Team A – Human Resources ExCo for financial services company

Prior to commencing the team inauguration forum and the monthly team coaching sessions, I facilitated a 90-minute coaching interview with each member of the ExCo. The original purpose of the ExCo coaching interviews was to provide clarity on the leaders' job roles, to have them articulate what is and what is not working for them, to identify how the senior leaders saw their core strengths and areas for development, and think about how the HR leadership team was experienced in the organisation.

The coaching interviews were designed to collect relevant data and impressions that staff held about the leadership team, the organisational culture, and to provide a chance for the staff to share their perceptions of Client A's culture and relationship system. I was already aware of a great deal of conflict between the senior executive leader of the team and members of the team. My aim was to develop trust and a relationship with each individual executive before commencing any team sessions. A further purpose was to understand the organisation's current functioning, aspirations from each of the managers for their own positions and to understand how clearly they understood their influence on the organisational system. On completion of the interviews, the core themes that had emerged were shared with the sponsors and the ExCo team which helped with the design of the overall intervention.

There was a wide variety of experience and expertise in the team, and a lack of confidence in the younger, less experienced members. It became clear that team members wanted to create an environment where their voices could be heard. They wanted to become a team where individuals would confidently voice their concerns, ask questions and professionally contribute to the more positive climate and culture in which they wished to work. They felt held back by the authoritarian and fear-driven culture. These interviews laid the foundation for going forward into the two-day team inauguration forum and the 12 monthly team coaching sessions.

Team B – Business Unit ExCo for medical scheme administrator

With Team B, I would be working with the general manager of the Business Unit, the Divisional Human Capital Executive for the holding company and the Organisational Development consultant for this ExCo. Following a range of meetings with my three sponsors, I sat in on an ExCo meeting and heard the results of a "Stress and Health" survey that had taken place across the organisation. The survey results revealed that a high per cent of managers and leaders were suffering from burn-out. This was a wake-up call for the organisation, and the team coaching for the ExCo team had been designed with this in mind.

Individual coaching interviews followed, as I met with each individual leader to understand their roles and responsibilities, and to build trust and rapport for the team coaching sessions. My initial sponsor and co-team coach (Deborah Williams) and I gave feedback to the other two sponsors in order to design the overall intervention. In the two-day team inauguration forum, the results were shared with the team.

This Business Unit was a guinea pig for team coaching across the organisation – and it was important to improve the ability to lead their respective teams, to increase their involvement with key organisational stakeholders, and their client, a large medical scheme. The team was working in deep silos, not taking responsibility and accountability for developing their teams, and cut off from the wider organisation. The client complaints system was in disarray, and the client was unhappy with the overall performance of the Business Unit. The most important goals for the team were to improve leadership performance, management of people and conflict, and to develop a network of relationships across the entire organisation and with the client.

Team C – IT company ExCo and staff

One of the key concerns that the ExCo had about the IT company was that it had grown rapidly from a small number of staff to over 20 people. Although there was great skill and expertise in the company, the ExCo completely lacked the management and leadership skills necessary to manage a growing staff complement. That led to unhappiness among the staff, who did not feel that they were properly briefed or supervised. There were administrators, technicians, consultants, managers and directors with no clear succession plan or talent development in place. The staff did not think there was enough diversity in the ExCo to represent them. This resulted in an unwieldy system with lack of clarity around job descriptions and roles – and little development of skills. Staff were expected to "get on with it", and sink or swim as had the directors themselves in their early careers. The ExCo still believed the company was like a "family" – but the system had broken down, with a lack of leadership and communication.

In order to understand what was happening in the system, Creina and I conducted coaching interviews with each member of the ExCo, and gave the ExCo an integrated report and feedback on results. This was followed by coaching interviews with each member of staff, and the integrated report and findings were first shared with the ExCo and then presented to and discussed with the entire staff. Decisions were made for the ExCo to have four or five coaching sessions to develop their leadership and management skill – and to create cohesion within the ExCo.

This was to be followed by several half-day team coaching sessions with leaders and staff to address the values and behaviours to which everyone could contribute – that would point the way ahead in how people would work together. Finally, all staff members were surveyed regarding the company's existing and desired values, to produce a summary report meant to be inclusive of every voice in the company, at all levels in the hierarchy. The coaching interview protocols for the ExCo and staff, and the values survey questionnaire are included in Appendices A–C, respectively.

Philosophies and models

My organisational team coaching has been influenced by systems thinking and eight models:

- Ernesto Spinelli's interpretation of Existential Phenomenology;
- Howard Guttman's Team Development Wheel;
- Patrick Lencioni's Five Dysfunctions of a Team Model;
- Nancy Kline's Thinking Environment® Methodology and Philosophy;
- Marita Fridjhon and Faith Fuller's Organisational Relationship Systems Coaching (ORSC™) underpinned by Relationship Systems Intelligence™;
- Hawkins' CID-CLEAR and Five Disciplines of Systemic Team Coaching;
- Hawkins' Systemic Team Coaching Model and
- Carr and Peters' Team Model and System.

Fridjhon and Fuller's ORSC Methodology is discussed in Chapter 7. The other seven models are explored in the following sections of this chapter.

Existential phenomenological approach

This investigates the significance, meaning and structure of the coaching intervention in the coach-client team conversation. Phenomenology is particularly suited to team coaching projects as it represents a quest for meaning: a search for the structure of the emerging phenomenon in the individual and team coaching conversations. Especially useful is the concept of bracketing and the emergence of assumptions (Spinelli, 1989).

During the coaching conversation, the process of asking questions has to be done from a point of no prejudgement or assumption, really clarifying and understanding the thinking of the client or the team member. This is difficult, as each individual operates within their own worldview and limiting paradigms, and each coach approaches the coaching conversation with their own assumptions and biases, and must therefore learn to bracket such assumptions and biases and put them aside. This is a core skill for a coach: to learn to bracket their own assumptions and biases. For example, if as a practitioner you are going to reframe or say something about the client's or the team's process, just describe it, do not impose your assumptions on what they are saying. This is a difficult but crucial point for a coach (Stout-Rostron, 2014: 113).

Existential phenomenology is used widely in psychotherapy models, but its origin is in philosophy. It has been employed in a number of areas, and explicitly in coaching. Phenomenology is appropriate to team coaching, as it helps the team coach to become aware of the processes that occur in, and the phenomena emerging from, the coach-client team conversation. This particular methodology assisted me in identifying useful intervention techniques (such as the Thinking Environment, ORSC and Lencioni's Five Dysfunctions of a Team). The model that emerged was a result of the work with my client teams.

An existential dilemma can potentially develop when the client feels their underlying value system clashes with that of their organisation. People usually have a strong sense of ethical, moral or faith-based values. When they voice their concerns inside a coaching assignment, they are often reflecting on where their value system is in conflict with the values of the organisation. Issues frustrating them may not be clear-cut, and are frequently complex. The issues raised could be related to performance ratings, recruitment procedures or even whether the organisation's actions are in alignment with its public claims. Business and team coaching should be aligned strategically with the overall values and objectives of an organisation. Existential dilemmas can arise during the coaching process if the executives need to make difficult choices incompatible with their own value system. This can impact individual team members and the team overall.

Guttman's Team Development Wheel

Howard Guttman's Team Development Wheel shows how a team can move through the stages of organisation and high performance if there is a team leader, team coach or facilitator to work with the team (Guttman, 2008: 82). There are four stages to his team coaching model: *testing, infighting, getting organised and high performance* (Guttman, 2008). These four stages have been adapted from Tuckman's model of group development (Figure 4.1), which said that the phases of forming, storming, norming and performing are necessary for a team to grow, face up to challenges, tackle problems, find solutions, plan work and deliver results (Tuckman, 1965).

Guttman explains that teams tend to be located within one of four stages of development (Guttman, 2009: 34), as illustrated in Figure 4.2. In Stage 1, the team is made up of underperformers, whereas in Stage 4, at the level of high performance, teams create clear goals and clear accountabilities (Guttman, 2009: 34). Stages 1 and 2 of the Team Development Wheel are about testing (Stage 1) and infighting (Stage 2).

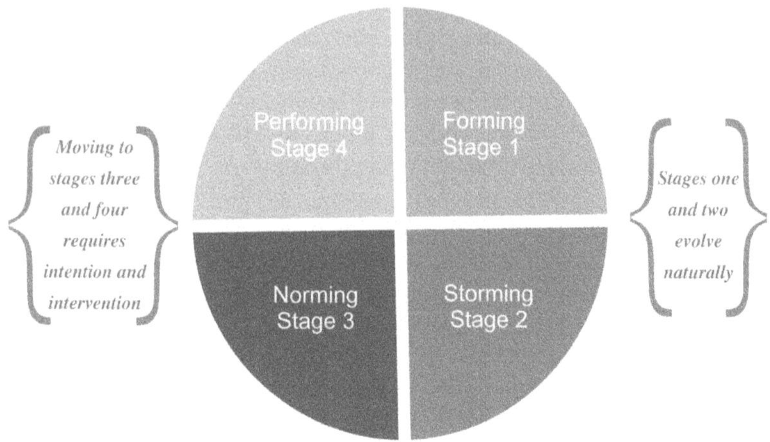

Figure 4.1 Tuckman's model of group development.
Source: Adapted from Tuckman (1965: 396).

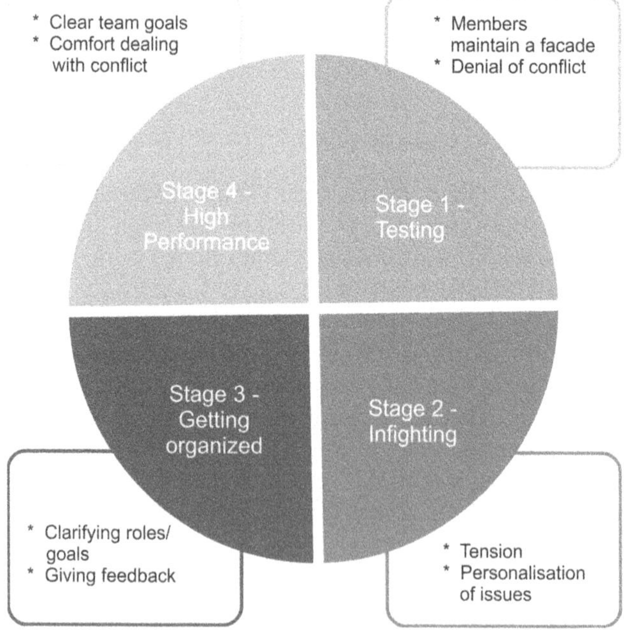

Figure 4.2 Guttman's Team Development Model.
Source: Pliopas, Kerr and Sosinski (2014: 11), adapted from Guttman (2008: 82).

He explains that it is rare for a team to move into Stage 3 without outside intervention, as the team needs to align on how they deal with conflict and how they communicate. Teams may fail to communicate due to differences in cultural heritage, and different cultures have very different levels of comfort with self-assertion (Guttman, 2009: 35–38).

The team experiences insight only when they work appropriately in Stages 3 and 4. In Stage 3, they typically clarify roles and goals, giving feedback to each other. And in Stage 4, they begin to create clear team goals and learn to manage different ways of dealing with conflict. The role of the coach is to support the team through each of the four stages, helping them to gain insights and create breakthroughs for their work with the team (Guttman, 2008). The coach can help the team to get organised in Stage 3 and begin to develop high performance in Stage 4. These new behaviours can become part of how they work together only if they have done their work in Stages 1 and 2 (testing and infighting).

Lencioni's Five Dysfunctions of a Team

Lencioni claims that an organisation is healthy only when it is whole, consistent and complete, and when its management, operations and culture are unified. "Healthy organisations outperform their counterparts, are free of politics and confusion and provide an environment where star performers never want to leave" (Lencioni, 2012). Lencioni's four disciplines for organisational health are as follows:

1 *Build a cohesive leadership team* – this stage is about getting the leaders to behave in a functional and cohesive way.
2 *Create clarity* – this stage is to ensure that members of the leadership team are intellectually aligned and clear on why the organisation exists and the priorities for the next few months.
3 *Over-communicate clarity* – this step is critical for behavioural and intellectual alignment. If leaders constantly repeat their message, it helps to reinforce what is true and important.
4 *Reinforce clarity* – this step means that simple human systems are used to enforce performance management and decision-making (Lencioni, 2012).

Everyone talks about teamwork, but rarely is it done effectively. Lencioni (2002) claims that his five pitfalls are what prevent most organisations from achieving teamwork. Building trust, courage, commitment, accountability and a proper focus on team goals takes time and effort. Leadership across the board is essential:

> The literature supports each of the five characteristics identified by Lencioni as predictors of team effectiveness. Empirical research shows a strong to very strong relationship between the five characteristics: trust, attention to results, commitment to the organisation, accountability, and dealing with conflict. The five characteristics are proven to be parts of each of the other characteristics, and are predictors of an effective team, as well.
>
> (Hamlin, 2008: iv)

Lencioni (2002) uses a leadership fable: a story of a technology company struggling to grow and find customers. Catherine Peterson is asked to come on board as a new CEO, and immediately recognises that the leadership team is not operating or functioning as a team – so the organisation is impacted negatively on all fronts, including customers, staff and products. The team struggles to think together and make decisions together. Its morale is at an all-time low. The five dysfunctions emerge in the telling of the fable – namely the lack of trust, the fear of conflict, lack of commitment, avoidance of accountability and inattention to results or focus on goals. Each function needs to be addressed separately. The model as it unfolds is that of Build Trust, Confront Conflict, Team Commitment, Take Accountability and Achieve Results. As Catherine addresses each dysfunction, some people leave the team, and others are brought on board.

Successful teamwork is not about adhering to theory, but about building common sense in alignment with discipline and persistence. The most important message is that teams succeed because they are *human*. By getting to know each other as individuals, with all the complexity that entails, the team can become more functional. This model is a very useful tool in working experientially. Lencioni (2002) defines a team as a relatively small number of people who share common goals as well as rewards and responsibilities for achieving them. However, the definition focuses primarily on the team and not necessarily on the wider system – the wider system must be introduced in working with the five stages of trust, conflict, commitment, accountability and results.

If there is an absence of trust, team members are unwilling to be vulnerable within the group. If there is a fear of conflict or confrontation, team members seek artificial harmony over constructive debate. If there is an absence of commitment, team members feign buy-in for group decisions, which creates ambiguity throughout the organisation. If there is an avoidance of accountability, ducking the obligation to call peers on their counterproductive behaviour sets low standards. Inattention to results and failure to focus on goals means attention is on personal objectives and success, the *status quo* and individual ego before team success. These dysfunctions are pervasive in all organisations and pinpoint the problems we often see when working with teams. But once they are identified, the team can address them.

The way that I introduce Lencioni's model is by asking the team to read or listen to the audio CD of Lencioni's (2002) book *The Five Dysfunctions of a Team*, and to complete the team diagnostic questionnaire. With each team, we work with all five dysfunctions of a team (trust, conflict, commitment, accountability and results) through a variety of my own experiential and ORSC™ exercises. There is also a field book and a facilitator's handbook, which are both available to work with the different techniques that Lencioni (2002) has identified. Particularly useful is his diagnostic questionnaire, which can be used to check the team's health. However, I tend to design my own experiential team activities to support the team in identifying where it is effective or ineffective (Figure 4.3).

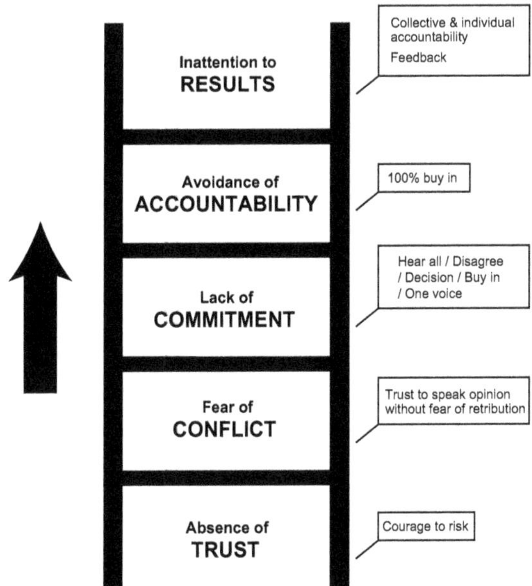

Figure 4.3 Lencioni's Five Dysfunctions of a Team Model.
Source: Adapted from Lencioni (2002: 188).

Kline's Thinking Environment philosophy and methodology

My work has been widely influenced by Nancy Kline's Thinking Environment philosophy and methodology. The underlying premise of Nancy Kline's Thinking Partnership is that the individual is best able to do their own thinking, and it provides a rigorous approach coaches can use to help to liberate their clients' thinking. The Thinking Partnership Model is useful for individual coaching. Kline's Transforming Meetings process, on the other hand, provides us with a set of tools that are undeniably among the best for team coaches: Rounds, Open Discussion, Thinking Pairs, Dialogue and Timed Talk – and two facilitated processes called Council and Transforming Meetings. The Thinking Partnership Coaching Model, the Council and the Transforming Meetings processes are underpinned by the Ten Components, ten specific behaviours that help individuals and teams to think for themselves and together. All of the following tools can be found in her book *Time to Think* (Kline, 1999).

Thinking Partnership Model®

The Thinking Partnership Model developed by Nancy Kline (1999) is arguably one of the purest, highest-level forms of coaching because it is completely non-directive. In most forms of best-practice coaching, the coach will directly intervene in the coaching conversation to help catalyse the manager's thinking, by asking a carefully considered and appropriate question that will "unlock" any confusion or blockages. In contrast, a Thinking Partner does not intervene directly in the coaching conversation at all. In fact, they ask only a limited and carefully defined range of neutral and non-directive questions.

This is because the key principle underpinning the Thinking Partnership Model is that the thinker is fully capable of thinking through the issue and working out the solution themselves. The critical role of the Thinking Partner is simply to provide a catalytic and supportive "thinking environment" within which the thinker is free to think *for* themselves – without interruption, prompting or "help". The only "help" offered is a series of questions to unlock limiting assumptions that may be blocking the thinker's thinking. The Thinking Partner or Coach is the catalyst for their thinking. I will first discuss Kline's new thinking around the individual Thinking Partnership Model, and then the team coach's work with the tools in the Council and Transforming Meetings processes (Figure 4.4).

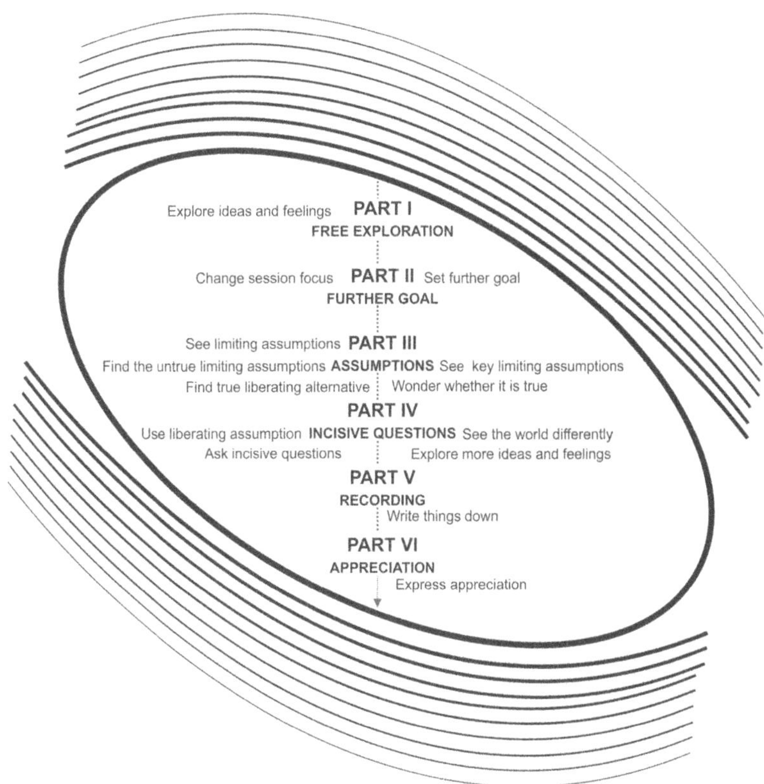

Figure 4.4 Kline's Thinking Partnership Model.
Source: Kline (2017: 4).

There are new discoveries in the development of Nancy Kline's Thinking Environment Model, which has emerged through consistent research and work in business and education since 1987. Kline's latest thinking is that "learning how to think for ourselves, and how to assist someone else to do that, is aligned with the very heart of life" (N. Kline, personal communication, 21 May 2018).

Kline's Six-Stage Individual Coaching Model has expanded and grown organically. Kline and the Time to Think faculty have continued to develop the individual coaching model based on what is needed on the part of the coachee/thinker, rather than what is needed on the part of the coach. During the first six months of 2018, Nancy Kline has continued to ask the question, "What does the thinker need next?" rather than "What question must the coach ask next?"

Kline makes it very clear that what the thinker needs determines what is required in terms of listening on the part of the coach. The purpose of a Thinking Partnership Session is for an individual to think for themselves, as far as they possibly can, about a topic of their choice. That changes the game of listening. She adds that "It is our work as Thinking Partners to provide the conditions for that, and only that" (N. Kline, personal communication, 21 May 2018). Her definition of a Thinking Environment is

> Getting the best from people means getting their best thinking. This means knowing how to offer them the highest-quality *attention*, how to ask *incisive questions*, how to recognise people's *strengths and achievements*, how to entice them beyond an addiction to certainty and into a *preference for responsible risk*. This is the creation of a thinking environment.
>
> (N. Kline, personal communication, 10 May 2018)

This is critical as a leaders' first job is to create a Thinking Environment. Leading today is a sophisticated process of articulating a vision compellingly – and getting the best from people so that their work manifests that vision.

Research shows that when training and developing coaches, we need to shift our focus from being the coach or thinking partner – and literally be able to "*think* as the partner". This is because the coach needs to always be trying to understand what "the mind in the other seems to need to stay independent as a thinker" (N. Kline, personal communication, May 21, 2018). Kline's focus is always on what the coachee or the thinker needs in order to *continue* to think independently – without input or distraction from the coach.

Kline's thinking is radical. Her observation is that the process of thinking is "ever-unfolding and discovering" and that we, as the Coach or the Thinking Partner, should be constantly observing the thinker. The thinker in ourselves as coach and the thinker in the other as coachee. Kline's concern is on *what the mind does when it is thinking* (N. Kline, personal communication, 21 May 2018). This means that we as coaches are always in the process of discovery of practice. The Thinking Environment in itself is always emerging, developing and creating. This has therefore led her to revisit her six-stage model.

In the six stages of the Thinking Partnership Model, Kline's explains that these questions are not simply part of an overarching structure of questions within linear stages. "The questions don't serve a superstructure of 'Parts' inside *boxes*.... The *questions* take place inside waves and serve *needs* that arise for the Thinker, who is still committed to the *purpose* of thinking independently". The questions to ask "follow logically from what the Thinker *needs, right then in order to keep thinking for themselves*". Kline suggests that essentially the stages and the boxes must go. "The questions and the needs they are precisely serving in the context of our singular purpose of independent thinking remain" (N. Kline, personal communication, 10 May 2018).

The question for the coach to ask is, "How far can a person go in their own thinking before they need mine?" Kline emphasises that it is *that question* which has driven the gradual discovery of the coaching session or thinking process from the very beginning, and it is that question which motivates the other questions at every juncture in the session (N. Kline, personal communication, 10 May 2018). The reference point for the Thinking Partner/Coach first and foremost must be to continually ask themselves: "In order to keep thinking for themselves, what does the Thinker need right now?" (N. Kline, personal communication, 10 May 2018). From the answer to that need and that question, the coach can ask the next question.

Her point is that the coach needs to ask the best possible question for generating a new wave of independent thinking. But the clues for what that question is likely to be, referring to the six stages of the coaching process, and in

> our knowledgeable speculation of what the mind, in order to start again, seems to do when it *pauses*. In two words: *Pauses rule*. The pause is the engine room of waves: it is the place of ignition of a new wave. It is teeming with fertility and speed-of-light processing.
> (N. Kline, personal communication, 2 June 2018)

Nancy is suggesting that we let go of the strict six-part structure of earlier versions of the Thinking Partnership Model with its implied linear sequence, and its "blind stampede" towards the key incisive question. This shift is intended to provide a new, and probably more accurate, depiction of what the human mind is doing to keep going when it is on an independent roll. That matters as it is exactly this process of igniting a new wave of thinking that we want to be able to emulate. "We want to be able to ask the questions the mind of the Thinker had been asking itself before it paused and could not generate a new wave, and so turned to us for help" (N. Kline, personal communication, 2 June 2018).

The question for the coach is, "What question will meet the client's need?" The body of the Thinking Partnership questions that have been discerned and tested over the past 30 years are still likely to provide the answers to that question. All that is changing is our understanding of how the mind gets to those questions so that we can reason our way to them for the Thinker if they ask us to:

> We get our clues for what that question is likely to be by using the body of knowledge of the Thinking Partnership® and in particular our knowledgeable speculation of what the mind, in order to start again, seems to do when it pauses.
>
> (N. Kline, personal communication, 2 June 2018)

What is the relevance to us as team coaches? A similar principle applies. In a team or group, the question we need to address as team coaches is, How do we help the team to keep *thinking independently and individually together?* And what does the team need now in order to keep thinking? As a team coach, you will need to be thinking about what your group need as thinkers *now* in order to keep thinking and to continue to generate new thinking.

Some of the questions in the Thinking Partnership Coaching Process are very useful in coaching a team to think through their issues and make decisions that need to be made. For example, to generate fresh thinking in the team, the team coach can ask the following:

- What are we assuming that is limiting our thinking on this issue right now?
- What else are we assuming that is stopping us from generating new thinking?
- What more do you think or feel or want to say?
- If we/you knew the answer, what might it be?

Team coaching tools from the Transforming Meetings process

The Transforming Meetings process includes what I consider the best tools to be used by a team coach when designing team coaching sessions. The underpinning of all of my team coaching sessions works with the basic principles of the Thinking Partnership model, and often with the applications from the Transforming Meetings and Council processes. That is, *how much further can the other person go in their thinking before they need my or anyone else's thinking?*

This is also a core principle when working with groups – how to help each one in the group to think in a wave, to pass the baton over to another for them to think in a wave and so on. One way to facilitate this process is to work in rounds to generate the group's thinking: that is, each one speaks once before anyone speaks twice – and no one speaks twice before everyone speaks once.

Rounds are a very dynamic way to open a team coaching session, setting a positive tone for the session and bringing everyone's voice into the room. Once everyone has spoken on the issue at hand, the team coach can facilitate an open discussion. Each of these processes are underpinned by the Ten Components of a Thinking Environment – that is, ten behaviours which enhance listening, attention and dialogue. The group can break into Thinking Pairs, Dialogue or Small Groups to focus on a particular issue or to generate more innovative thinking before bringing those new ideas back into the plenary group. I give more information on all of these building blocks below.

BUILDING BLOCKS

The building blocks of the Transforming Meetings® process help to build "communication muscle" in a team. This includes Rounds, Open Discussion, Thinking Pairs, Dialogue, the Council Process and agenda items as Questions – all of which are underpinned by the Ten Components or behaviours. Working with these tools means that individual team members adapt their experience to learn how to better manage themselves and to lead others, improving decision-making, adapting and connecting to build alliances with each other and ultimately with key stakeholders.

TEN COMPONENTS

At the outset of working with a team, I usually introduce the Ten Components. As we design our work together, we eventually create a Designed Team Alliance or a Team Charter with the team's own selected behaviours that they wish to work to going forward. But to start with, I help to create a Thinking Environment by introducing them to these ten ways of "being together", ten ways of treating each other or ten ways of thinking together. The idea behind the Ten Components is that you as the team coach are setting up the right conditions for people to be willing to think for themselves within the group and with each other. These Ten Components are powerful – but each one operates individually, as well as a system. The Ten Components are as follows:

1 Attention

According to Kline, "listening with palpable respect and interest and without interruption means that the quality of your attention profoundly affects the quality of the other person's thinking" (Kline, 2017: 5). Giving this kind of attention brings to life that which was not present before, that is, a promise of no interruption. But it is important that we set boundaries with each other in the group, such as how much time each speaker will take, or if working in Thinking Pairs, how much time each thinker has to think and speak.

2 Equality

This means "treating each other as thinking peers, giving equal turns and attention, keeping agreements and boundaries" (Kline, 2017: 5). Kline makes it very clear that even within a hierarchy, people can be equal as thinkers. It is true that some people can talk you into a coma, which is why we need to set boundaries of time. It means everyone gets a turn – which is the core principle of rounds. Everyone matters, everyone has a chance to speak at least once on an issue and to think equally. If the group moves from a round into open discussion, you as the team coach can always move back into a round if two or three voices begin to dominate.

3 Ease

Ease simply means "offering freedom from internal rush or urgency. Ease creates, and urgency destroys. When it comes to helping people think for themselves, sometimes doing means not doing" for them (Kline, 2017: 5). It seems like we gain time when we are in a hurry. But ease is counter-intuitive, counter-cultural and counter-experience (Kline, 2017). Rushing and feeling urgent are the norms, but actually take more time with everyone interrupting each other, and not letting each one finish their thoughts to be built upon organically within the team.

4 Appreciation

Appreciation means just that – "offering genuine acknowledgement of a person's qualities, and practising a five-to-one ratio of appreciation to criticism. The human mind thinks more rigorously and creatively in a context of concrete, genuine praise". Neuroscience research has gone into the importance of appreciation for individuals and teams. What appreciation offers the team is that it develops an individual and organisational culture of acknowledgement and appreciation.

The Gottman Institute in Seattle has been researching the importance of appreciation in relationships for many years (Gottman, 2003). Research by the HeartMath Institute also shows that when we experience heartfelt emotions such as appreciation, love, care and compassion, the heart produces a very different rhythm – one that has a smooth pattern and looks something like gently rolling hills. Scientists consider harmonious, or smooth heart rhythms, which are indicative of positive emotions, to be indicators of cardiovascular efficiency and nervous-system balance (HeartMath Institute, 2018).

5 Encouragement

Encouragement builds the confidence and self-esteem of the other. It means "giving courage to go to the cutting edge of ideas by moving beyond internal competition, and it means that to be better than another is not necessarily to be good" (Kline, 2017: 5). Encouragement means giving courage to someone to go the edge of their thinking – and it requires you as a Thinking Partner to stop competing with the Thinker. Instead, we choose to champion each other's thinking.

6 Feelings

In the working world, we tend to think we have to suppress our emotions and feelings – not allowing them to interfere with our rational or logical thinking. However, the way our brain is hardwired, we cannot think without feeling, nor can we feel without thinking. This behaviour does not mean we are meant to shout, scream or cry – it simply means that we need to "allow sufficient emotional release to restore thinking". Although this may seem peculiar, it means that we need to be connected to our feelings and emotions in order to think something through. And it means being able to sit with someone who is emotional, without infantilising them, and letting them explore their thoughts and their feelings on an issue. One of the things that happens in team coaching is that people become willing to share their real stories – and to feel safe rather than vulnerable in the group.

7 Information

Information is about supplying the facts, or the necessary information. In Kline's research, it means "dismantling denial" (Kline, 2017: 6). This does not mean we step into the thinker's space and automatically give them the information they need. It is up to them to determine how much input they require from you. Without the appropriate information, it may not be possible for the thinker to work through a problem or an issue. It is important that members of a team or group not hoard information and deny information to others if it would help with decision-making. If we can recognise that denial is the withdrawal of information, then we offer each other the dismantling of denial.

8 Diversity

Diversity means welcoming all of our own identities and being proud of our identities. It is only then that we can speak as ourselves, communicating from whom we really are. Kline has indicated, "we can think for ourselves only if we think as ourselves". She explains, "diversity is about welcoming diverse thinking and diverse group identities. The mind works best in the presence of reality, and reality is diverse. Homogeneity is a thinking inhibitor" (Kline, 2017: 6). In any team you are coaching, there will be a myriad of identities and thinking in the room which need to be acknowledged and welcomed. It is helping the team to hear each other.

9 Incisive questions

Incisive questions are a crucial behaviour that support thinking. These questions help to replace an untrue, limiting assumption (lived as if it were true) with a "true" liberating assumption, and connecting that liberating assumption to the thinker's goal. Incisive questions "remove assumptions that limit our ability to think for ourselves clearly and creatively" (Kline, 2017: 6). And "right inside an Incisive Question lies the liberation of the human mind" (Kline, 2009: 86).

Cognitive behavioural therapy helps us to understand assumptions. An assumption is a proposition that one takes for granted is true without examining the relevant facts. Assumptions are positioned mid-way between automatic thoughts and core beliefs. They act as a translation between the two. They are sometimes known as *intermediate beliefs*. *Automatic thoughts* are on the surface, and are like short tapes that flash through your mind. They are actually a form of self-talk which you use throughout the day. *Core beliefs* develop over time, usually from childhood. They tend to be strongly held, rigid and inflexible: often the very essence of how we see ourselves and other people. *Core beliefs* focus on information that supports a belief and ignores evidence that contradicts that belief – and they are hard to shake.

10 Place

Our environment needs to say back to people "You matter". There are two *places* we need to acknowledge. There is the environment in which we live and work. And there is the place where we do our own thinking, inside our own bodies. This means we need to nourish and take care of our health in order to think for ourselves. "When the physical environment affirms your importance, you think more boldly, and when your body is cared for and respected, your thinking improves" (Kline, 2017: 6).

ROUNDS

Each individual team member learns how to organically develop ideas working in a "round", and to actively listen to and hear one another one-on-one and in the plenary group. It is tough to start with as they will be actively experiencing a completely new way of interacting with each other.

There is no doubt that rounds at first seem weird to participants. Each one speaks once before anyone speaks twice, and nobody speaks twice before everyone has spoken once. Once everyone has spoken twice the group can move into open discussion. It is also important that in the plenary group everyone keeps their attention focused on the person speaking, not on their own note taking, cell phones or iPad. In this way, the group stays disciplined, actively listening to the thinking of their peers. "Your important thought becomes *archaic* and way off base by the time it is your turn. As you go round the group, your new thinking has already emerged" (Kline, 2017: 8).

The purpose of the round is that it brings everyone's voice into the room on a particular issue, or as you get started in your team coaching session. It is useful to time each person – say give each one two minutes for the check-in – after asking them a positive question. Such as "What do you most want for yourself from today, and what is your wish for the team?" Or "What did you most value for yourself from our last session, and in what way have your colleagues seen some kind of positive change in you?" Or "Of all the behaviours we identified in our Designed Team Alliance/Team Charter, which most resonate with you, how do you currently demonstrate them and which behaviour do you most need to work on?"

THINKING PAIRS

The reason for developing Thinking Pairs in a team is to be able to develop a "peer coaching" process within the team so that team members can think together on a regular basis outside of the team coaching sessions – building relationship intelligence and creating a network of thinking clusters within the business.

Each person speaks on a topic of their choice to the other person. But most important is that there is no *content response* to the other – which makes it very different from having a conversation. In fact you are *thinking or having a think*, and with the thinking pair you do not need the other person to think for you. Thinking Pairs are relatively easy because the *strangeness* of the lack of content response from the Thinking Partner keeps the discipline in place.

Thinking pairs are a tool in your team coaching sessions and in the client's meetings. You can ask the members of the team to each write down any business issues or challenges they are facing, and identify the question that sits inside each topic. Then, you can put them into thinking pairs to each share their topic and the question they wish to address. When a team is cycling around an issue, and not able to clarify their thinking, or if several people are dominating the discussion, a question to ask the team and then split them into pairs could be the following:

- What are we assuming that is getting in our way or stopping us from reaching a decision?

Other examples of questions for thinking pairs are as follows:

- Which of our chosen behaviours do we have in place in this team, and which do we need to work on?
- What works well in your meetings, and what goes wrong?

When each thinking pair is complete, having given both a chance to think, it is very useful to have each partner acknowledge and appreciate the other. They can simply answer the question, "What quality or characteristic do you appreciate about the other that they bring into the team and the business?" Appreciations at the end of a team coaching session, at the end of a thinking pair or at the end of a meeting build the muscles of empathy, encouragement and validation of the other.

DIALOGUE

Working with dialogue tests the equality and diversity in a team. The back and forth of dialogue is easier and more familiar than working in a thinking pair – because it feels more like a conversation. But it is not a conversation; it is thinking together by having a wave of thought and passing the *thinking baton* over to the other. Dialogue is a greater challenge than a thinking pair, where it is easy to interrupt the other's thinking. Interrupting fragments and distracts the attention of the other.

Where in open discussion it is very familiar to pass the baton over, often egos get in the way and the baton does not get passed equally among team members. In dialogue, there are only two people thinking together – as opposed to two people talking together. The exchange is two-way, and it takes responsibility to stop your own turn and pass the *baton* over to the other. Kline (2011: 12) describes dialogue as

> thinking pairs on the same topic with short, frequent turns back and forth. And for dialogue to be rich, intelligent and worth the time, the Ten Components need to be offered to each other. To hold the quality of dialogue, the two thinkers need to trust that the other will not interrupt.

THE COUNCIL PROCESS

The Council Process provides the forum for discussing a key issue for the team in a team coaching session. There are often numerous issues to be discussed. Several of those issues could become part of the Transforming Meetings process. Working with the Council Process means agreeing on a topic critical for the team, but may be owned or managed by one of its members. Often emerging from work done earlier in your team coaching session. This works for a leader, or a member of the team, who wishes to get the best thinking from the team, but without being told what to do. A member of the team chairs the process. Whoever owns the topic presents to the group.

Kline (2017) explains that the Council session is where a member of the team wishes to solve a problem or think through an issue, and wants the best thinking from each member of the team. It is a way of acknowledging the team's "experience, knowledge and information" – without being told what to think yourself. The Council Process "allows the wisdom of the group to unobtrusively make its way into the problem-solving of one person" (Kline, 2017: 23).

Hawkins' CID-CLEAR and Five Disciplines of Systemic Team Coaching

In *Leadership Team Coaching*, Peter Hawkins (2014) explains that strong leadership teams are critical to organisational success, and that to develop successful teams, the use of the Five Disciplines of team coaching – *commissioning, clarifying, co-creating, connecting* and *core learning* – can help leaders to define needs, measure results and create a contract describing the team's goals for the coaching process. The coach is a *partner* to the team and helps leaders work on business transformations while they manage day-to-day operations.

Leadership team coaching focuses on the behaviour of the team more than on the work of its individual members. Finding the right coach for a specific team is an important challenge. Hawkins advocates helping the client to envision what they hope to get from team coaching; then soliciting and selecting candidates; conducting a "contracting" phase to develop mutual expectations; and allowing for regular reviews and a final evaluation. Creating a leadership team capable of transforming an organisation requires time and passion. He defines a team as "a small number of people with complementary skills who are committed to a common purpose, set of performance goals and shared approach for which they hold themselves mutually accountable" (Hawkins, 2014: 36). Team members must commit to change, believe in the organisation, hold strong values, learn continuously, handle uncertainty and possess vision and courage.

To initiate the team coaching process, Hawkins (2014) advocates using the CID-CLEAR model. The CID-CLEAR model reveals the role a coach plays in leading a team in each of the Five Disciplines noted below. In CID-CLEAR, I found the two stages of contracting and inquiry extremely helpful in working with my case study client Team B, a medical scheme administrator:

- *Contracting 1* – The coach holds an initial discussion about the team's understanding of coaching, and everyone works towards an agreement about what the coach's job entails.
- *Inquiry* – In this data-gathering phase, the coach learns about how the team works.
- *Diagnosis and design* – The coach analyses the data from the first two steps.
- *Contracting 2* – The coach and the team create a contract describing the team's goals for the coaching process.
- *Listening* – The coach examines the issues identified in the previous step while remaining alert to verbal and non-verbal feedback.
- *Explore and experiment* – The coach and the team construct new ways of behaving that address the issues they've identified.
- *Action* – The team takes the knowledge it has gained and puts it into practice, sometimes using SMART (specific, measurable, actionable, realistic and timely) action steps.
- *Review* – In this final step, the coach and team examine how the process unfolded and make plans for the next stages (Hawkins, 2014: 86–103).

Hawkins' high-performing transformational teams

Tichy and Devanna (1986, cited in Hawkins, 2014: 39) define the seven characteristics of the transformational leader as follows:

- They clearly see themselves as change agents.
- They are courageous.
- They believe in people.
- They are driven by a strong set of values.
- They are lifelong learners.
- They can cope with complexity, uncertainty and ambiguity.
- They are visionaries.

According to Hawkins (2014), a successful team needs to practise the five key disciplines of transformational leadership: *commissioning*, *clarifying*, *co-creating*, *connecting* and *reflecting on core learning*. He advocates that a leadership team must consider the company's tasks and processes and the coming together of internal and external concerns. This requires practising five cyclical disciplines:

1 *Commissioning* – Team members define the team's purpose and determine how it will measure success. To coach a team in the commissioning stage, the coach gathers data about the goals of the company's transformation plan, how the team enacted the plan and what the members thought of the results.
2 *Clarifying* – The team develops and defines its mission, goals, values and processes. In this stage, the coach helps the team scrutinise why it operates, where the company focuses, what values underpin the business and what the team hopes to become. This discussion helps team members to own their goals and prepare to execute the resulting plan.
3 *Co-creating* – The team monitors how it functions as a whole, celebrates its achievements and corrects any failures. To achieve co-creation, the coach looks at the team's objectives and the measures it uses to assess success. The team coach can observe meetings or help the team members process the results of their work to help them stay on track.
4 *Connecting* – The team focuses on how each member connects with external stakeholders. In the connecting phase, the coach helps team members look outward to see how the members of the organisation perceive the team's goals and results.

5 *Core learning* – Team members assess their performance and draw lessons from their experience. The coach gives the team members feedback on their performance and what they can change in the future (Hawkins, 2014: 45–51).

Leaders often set goals within their leadership teams, but have trouble communicating those objectives within the wider organisational system. To guarantee core learning, the coach helps the team learn as a collective while avoiding pitfalls such as working by trial and error, focusing on the past, emphasising theory or analysis without action or expecting the organisation to execute the team's plans without change or comment (Figure 4.5).

Coaching a team, rather than individuals, requires attending more to the team than to any one member, also the mind-set of a sports team coach. The team coach must understand his or her team members and the company's processes. According to Hawkins (2011), team coaches must develop nine capacities:

1 *Self-awareness* – Understand the team's verbal and non-verbal cues.
2 *Self-ease* – Don't worry about proving yourself.

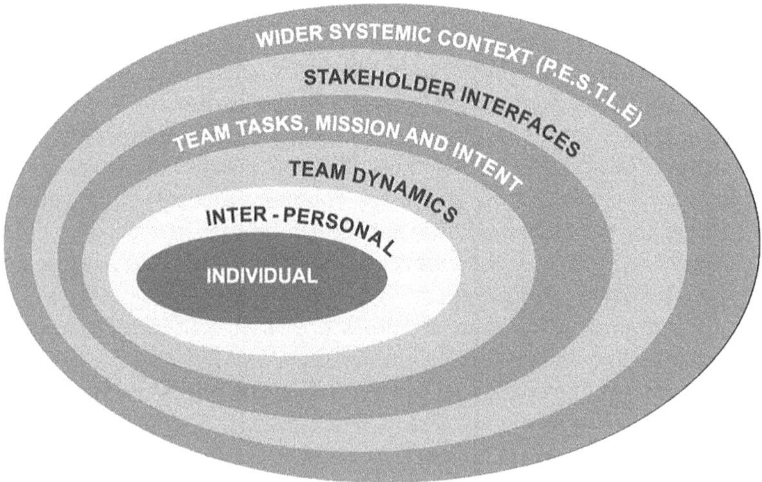

Figure 4.5 The wider systemic context of Hawkins' Systemic Team Coaching Model.

Source: Hawkins (2016: 70).

3 *Stay in the partnership zone* – Serve as the team's partner, not its boss or subordinate. Do not "fall into deference or ... arrogance".
4 *Use appropriate authority, presence and impact* – Lead firmly to help the team accomplish its work.
5 *Relationship engagement* – Relate to the other members on your team as much as possible.
6 *Encourage* – Help inspire team members and instil "appropriate enthusiasm".
7 *Work across differences* – Help others manage their varied cultural expectations, whether from working in another department or in another country.
8 *Ethical maturity* – Develop a strong ethical and moral base, and exercise it when the team needs guidance.
9 *A sense of humour and humility* – Laugh at yourself and recognise your fallibility (Hawkins, 2011: 157–158).

Carr and Peters' Team Coaching Model and System

According to Carr and Peters (2013: 82), practitioners have contributed to the team coaching literature by providing a number of case studies and models for facilitating team coaching conversations. These case studies document the benefits and outcomes that team coaching participants themselves identified, including increased learning, decision-making, information sharing, communication and participation (Carr and Peters, 2013: 82).

According to Hackman (2012), the three key drivers for improved team performance are as follows:

1 team design and structure;
2 team launch and
3 ongoing team coaching.

Wageman, Fisher and Hackman (2009) categorised 120 teams into high, mediocre and poor performance, and analysed the differentiating factors between groups. They created a model that outlined three essential and three enabling conditions for team effectiveness. Essential conditions are *creating a real team, having a compelling purpose* and *putting the right people on the team.* The essential conditions are considered to be the basic building blocks for a senior team. These three elements work together when implementing changes in a senior leadership team. If a team changes one of the essentials, it is important to re-scrutinise the other two at the same time.

The enabling conditions are having a *solid structure, within a supportive context*, and *engaging in a competent team coaching process*. The enabling conditions are said to accelerate progress, improve effectiveness and help the team to deliver outstanding results. The researchers suggest that the essentials must be adequately in place before undertaking the enabling conditions.

I was influenced by the high-performance team coaching model and system of Peters and Carr (2013), as the structure of my team coaching model emerged throughout 2012–2016 in the team coaching sessions with my three client case studies. In their study, the researchers documented and compared the experience of team coaching between their two leadership teams using a qualitative case study methodology that tracked the participants' experiences.

The Carr and Peters system (2013: 91) highlights three team coaching stages (team beginning, mid-point and end), and three overarching team coaching functions (define and initiate, review and re-align, and reassess and integrate). They have proposed a new, six-stage High-Performance Team Coaching Model that can be used by leaders and team coaches alike (see Figure 4.6).

On the outside of the circle, they have aligned the three main coaching functions with the natural beginning, mid-point and ending team stages. The three coaching functions are matched to the team's stage: (1) define and initiate at the beginning; (2) review and realign at the mid-point and (3) integrate at the end of a team's cycle. The arrows indicate the natural progression of the team's stages. Similar to my model, Carr and Peters' (2013) system has a strong focus on coaching teams at the beginning of a new team cycle in order to set up the team conditions from the beginning, and to launch or inaugurate the team.

There are six stages to Carr and Peters' (2013) system – *assessment, coaching for team design, team launch, individual coaching, ongoing team coaching, review learning and successes*. They have included team effectiveness in their system as the key outcome of team coaching. Carr and Peters' (2013: 95) six-phase High-Performing Team Coaching System was developed based on case study results and a literature review of methods and strategies that were found to promote team performance. The authors recognise that in real-life practice, only one or more may be applied by the team coach. However, according to Carr and Peters (2013), each of these stages is important to team success.

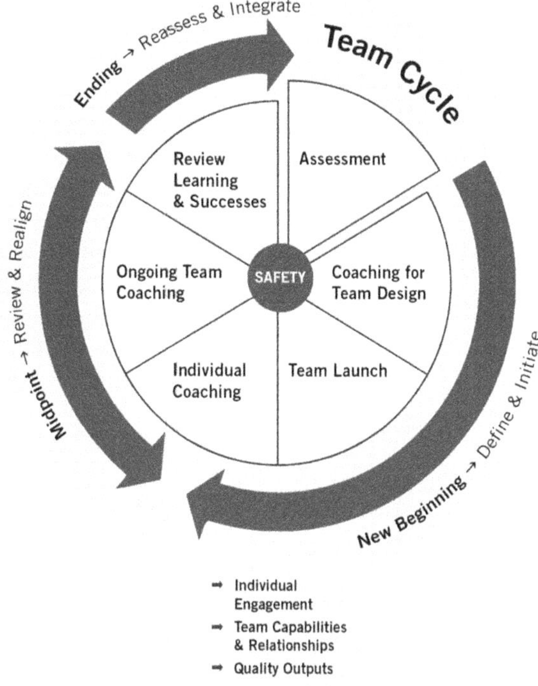

Figure 4.6 Carr and Peters' Team Coaching System.
Source: Peters and Carr (2013).

Conclusion

A team coach plays multiple roles. First, to focus on individual members of the team, enabling them to develop self-awareness about their own attitudes, assumptions, behaviours and perspectives. As part of this process, individual coaching is often offered in alignment with the team coaching intervention. Second is the focus on the team as a system. Third, wearing a systemic hat, the coach brings into focus the wider system, which includes the community within which the organisation works, customers/clients, suppliers, senior executives/managers/team leaders, all other employees and organisational stakeholders. This puts a focus on the larger objectives of the organisation, and on the *network of relationships* which impacts the team and the organisation's business processes.

Team coaching should be practical and experiential. The coach enables the team to build a Thinking Environment in their monthly team sessions together, creating a level of safety in order to have robust conversations while learning to manage conflict effectively, with each leader taking responsibility for their leadership behaviours and living the values of the organisation. This means leaders learning from their own experience to better manage themselves and lead others, adapting and connecting to build alliances with each other and ultimately with all key stakeholders. Building relationships, being authentic communicators, engaging positively with each other, making decisions and managing how to structure and facilitate meetings are the secret of success at every level in business: this should be our focus in all team coaching sessions.

References

Abrahamson, D. (2016). *Team Coaching: Why, Where, When and How*. WABC White Paper, Best Fit Business Coaching Series. Saanichton, BC: WABC Coaches.

Carr, C., and Peters, J. (2013). The experience of team coaching: A dual case study. *International Coaching Psychology Review*, 8(1):80–98.

Gottman, J. (2003). *The Seven Principles for Making Marriage Work: A Practical Guide from the Country's Foremost Relationship Expert*. London: Orion.

Guttman, H.M. (2008). *Great Business Teams: Cracking the Code for Breakthrough Performance*. Hoboken, NJ: Wiley.

Guttman, H.M. (2009). Conflict management as a core competency for HR professionals. *People and Strategy*, 32(1):32–39.

Hackman, J.R. (2012). From causes to conditions in group research. *Journal of Organisational Behaviour*, 26:37–74.

Hamlin, J.L. (2008). *Team Effectiveness: A Validation Study of Lencioni's Five Functions of a Team*. Unpublished D.Ed. dissertation. La Verne, CA: College of Education and Organisational Leadership, University of La Verne.

Hawkins, P. (2011). *Leadership Team Coaching: Developing Collective Transformational Leadership*. London: Kogan Page.

Hawkins, P. (2014). *Leadership Team Coaching: Developing Collective Transformational Leadership*. Second Edition. London: Kogan Page.

Hawkins, P. (2016). *Systemic Team Coaching Certificate Programme Workbook*. London: Academy of Executive Coaching. Peter Hawkins, Renewal Associates/AoEC Diploma Programme in Systemic Team Coaching. URL: www.renewalassociates.co.uk & www.aoec.com.

HeartMath Institute. (2018). *An Appreciative Heart Is Good Medicine*. URL: www.heartmath.org/articles-of-the-heart/personal-development/an-appreciative-heart-is-good-medicine/. Accessed 10 July 2018.

Kline, N. (1999). *Time to Think: Listening to Ignite the Human Mind.* London: Cassell Illustrated.

Kline, N. (2009). *More Time to Think: A Way of Being in the World.* Pool-in-Wharfedale: Fisher King.

Kline, N. (2011). *Transforming Meetings.* Workbook. Wallingford, UK: Time to Think.

Kline, N. (2017). *The Thinking Partnership.* Workbook. Wallingford, UK: Time to Think.

Lencioni, P. (2002). *The Five Dysfunctions of a Team: A Leadership Fable.* San Francisco, CA: Jossey-Bass.

Lencioni, P. (2012). *The Advantage: Why Organisational Health Trumps Everything Else in Business.* San Francisco, CA: Jossey-Bass.

McWhinney, W. (1993). *Paths of Change: Strategic Choices for Organisations and Society.* Thousand Oaks, CA: Sage.

McWhinney, W., Webber, J.B., Smith, D.M., and Novokowsky, B.J. (1996). *Creating Paths of Change: Managing Issues and Resolving Problems in Organisations.* Venice, CA: Enthusion.

Peters, J., and Carr C. (2013). *High Performance Team Coaching: A Comprehensive System for Leaders and Coaches.* Victoria, BC, Canada: Friesen Press.

Pliopas, A., Kerr, A.B., and Sosinski, M. (2014). *Team Coaching Project.* Unpublished Master Coach Programme assignment. Santa Barbara, CA: Hudson Institute of Coaching.

Spinelli, E. (1989). *The Interpreted World: An Introduction to Phenomenological Psychology.* London: Sage.

Stout-Rostron, S. (2014). *Leadership Coaching for Results: Cutting-Edge Techniques for Coach and Client.* Johannesburg: Knowres.

Tichy, N.M., and Devanna, M.A. (1986). *The Transformational Leader.* New York, NY: Wiley.

Tuckman, B.W. (1965). Developmental sequence in small groups. *Psychological Bulletin*, 63(6):384–399.

Wageman, R., Fisher, C.M., and Hackman, J.R. (2009). Leading teams when the time is right: Finding the best moments to act. *Organisational Dynamics*, 38(3):192–203.

5 Diversity and culture in teams

Sunny Stout-Rostron

Defining culture

"Culture may be defined as a collective programming of the mind that shows in the values, symbols and rituals to which we hold fast" (Hofstede, 2001). In recent decades, significant changes have taken place in the way the world is organised, thought about and represented – none more so than in the increasing sensitivity to cultural diversity. Matsumoto (1996: 16) defines culture as "the set of attitudes, values, beliefs, and behaviours shared by a group of people, but different for each individual, communicated from one generation to the next".

Spencer-Oatey (2008: 3) suggests that

> culture is a fuzzy set of basic assumptions and values, orientations to life, beliefs policies, procedures and behavioural conventions that are shared by a group of people, and that influence (but do not determine) each member's behaviour and his/her interpretations of the 'meaning' of other people's behaviour.

Culture has also been defined as "a set of beliefs and values about what is desirable and undesirable in a community of people, and a set of formal or informal practices to support the values" (Javidan and House, 2001: 292).

Hofstede's (1980) research examined culture using surveys of 88,000 IBM employees worldwide to classify 40 nations along four cultural dimensions (to which Hofstede added a fifth in 2001):

1 *Power distance* – the relationship with authority and social inequality;
2 *Individualism versus collectivism* – the relationship between the individual and the group;

3. *Masculinity versus femininity* – the tendency towards assertiveness in contrast to modesty;
4. *Avoidance of uncertainty* – the control of aggression and expressions of emotions and
5. *Long-term versus short-term orientation* (Barak, 2014: 176–177; Egan and Bendick, 2008: 388; Hofstede, 1980).

Robbins (2001) attests that a flaw in most organisational behaviour research is that it is chiefly (80 per cent) conducted by Americans in the United States. Hofstede's original research included South Africa, but because the respondents were primarily English-speaking white males, the research was hardly representative of the population. Although strongly Eurocentric, Hofstede's dimensions are internationally recognised as descriptive of regional, ethnic and religious cultures (Schneier, 1998).

In 1998, Schneier conducted qualitative research in South Africa to determine whether these dimensions are sufficiently relevant and appropriate to describe South African ethnic culture. Her results indicate that, although relevant, Hofstede's five dimensions are not sufficient to describe South African ethnicity. Values that are distinctly African emerged in two main areas: communalism and procedure-driven time orientation. Communalism is described as implying an interdependence of a uniquely African kind; it stands separate from individualism and collectivism. Schneier (1998: 223) argues that acknowledging an African procedural-traditional time orientation may play a role in focusing on the quality of an experience or intervention and its results, in addition to maintain efficiency within the traditional Western linear time orientation.

Organisational culture

In *Coaching on the Axis*, Kahn (2014: 21) introduces the notion that business exists within a distinct cultural context which is characterised by market forces. He advocates that all coaches start with the cultural context as their starting point, developing an understanding of the phenomenon of culture, and particularly corporate or organisational culture. He explains that the generalist view of culture aligns well with systems thinking, and describes culture as emerging from social interactions, and being the result of shared symbols and meanings (Kahn, 2014: 22):

> Culture is the intrinsic social fabric through which organisation occurs, consciously and unconsciously, intentionally and unintentionally. Culture provides the code that allows human beings to

> predict behaviour, maintain relationships, and find meaning and purpose, it supplies us our language, which facilitates the meaning structure for living. Culture is ultimately the foundation of our social order.
>
> (Kahn, 2014: 22–23)

Kahn works with Schein's definition of organisational culture:

> a pattern of shared basic assumptions that was learned by a group as it solved its problems of *internal adaptation* and *external adaptation*, that has worked well enough to be considered valid and, therefore, to be taught to new members as the correct way to perceive, think, and feel in relation to those problems.
>
> (Schein, 2004: 17, quoted in Kahn, 2014: 26–27, emphasis in original)

According to Schein, in relation to external adaptation, and managing to cope with change, there are essential elements that need to be maintained: *mission and strategy, goals, means, measurement, correction*. The essential elements to maintain internal relationships are to create a common language and conceptual categories; defining group boundaries and criteria for inclusion and exclusion; distributing power and status; developing norms of intimacy, friendship and love; defining and allocating rewards and punishments and explaining the unexplainable, for example, ideology and religion (Schein, 2010: 88, 111–112, cited in Kahn, 2014: 27–28). Deal and Kennedy declared that "every business – in fact every organisation – has a culture" (Deal and Kennedy, 2000: 4, quoted in Kahn, 2014: 28) because business is a social system which organises behaviour with the objective of succeeding in a competitive landscape.

Kahn explains that Schein examines the relationship between culture and leadership – maintaining that neither can be understood without the other (Schein, 2004, cited in Kahn, 2014: 29). "Leadership is seen as the act of influencing and shaping the behaviour and values of others thereby creating the conditions for new culture formation, whereas management is seen to be the activity that operationally sustains the existing system" (Kahn, 2014: 29).

Important for team coaches, is that when culture is dysfunctional, leadership is the tool the team can use to unlearn difficult cultural assumptions, and to develop ways of adapting and being more effective. Both leaders and team coaches need to understand the deeper levels of a culture – organisational and societal – to understand the assumptions on which the group is operating; some assumptions may be liberating and true while others may be limiting and untrue.

Cultural competence in coaching

Coaches need to understand what, when, how and how much culture matters in practical, interpersonal and organisational situations. To manage intergroup conflict, we need to equip managers and leaders to understand "how cultural differences work" and "how to turn cultural competence into a competitive advantage". Consequently, the following personal competences are important for managers: flexibility, resourcefulness, tolerance for ambiguity, vision, cultural self-awareness, cultural consciousness and multicultural leadership (Egan and Bendick, 2008: 387).

Cultural competence is defined as a "set of congruent behaviours, attitudes, and policies that come together in a system, agency, or among professionals, enabling them to work effectively in cross-cultural situations" (Cross, Bazron, Dennis and Isaacs, 1989: iv–v). It starts with managers' personal cultural intelligence, or ability to operate in a variety of situations, whether they arise from cross-functional assignments within a company, diverse work teams or foreign postings (Earley and Mosakowski, 2004: 2).

The role of the culturally aware team coach is to explore and develop self-awareness around each team member's deeply held assumptions and paradigms about themselves, and about others who are different to them. A combination of coaching and intercultural skills is essential not only for leaders but also for the team coaches who will be able to facilitate development of each team member's potential.

For the team coach, the ability to integrate the cultural dimension into their coaching style means that they will be able to help their clients unleash more human potential and achieve more meaningful objectives. As the client becomes more aware of cultural differences, the latter can be used constructively to provide for learning, growth and more effective interpersonal communications and relationships.

To be able to do this, coach practitioners need to question their own views of the world and develop an acute awareness of the complex processes – social, cultural, economic and personal – that make up who and what they are.

Due to a technologically more connected world, organisations are having to deal with increasing diversity and with multiculturalism, gender and quality initiatives. Organisations are being asked to embrace diversity to improve performance at every level from the factory floor to executive level. According to Christian, Porter and

Moffitt (2006: 460), the objective of diversity management is to "increase our understanding of the effects that work group diversity has on cohesion and performance". But while "there is general consensus among researchers as to what constitutes diversity management, there is little agreement on the effect that it has in the workplace".

One of the clear functions of the team coach is to understand the culture, values and relationship systems within the workplace, and to know what the accepted standards of diverse cultural influences are. Recent research suggests the need to develop a theoretical framework to provide guidelines in culturally diverse contexts. In developing their own integrative approaches to team coaching, coaches should consider their own experience and training, and choose theoretical models that will suit a wide range of clients.

Inclusion versus exclusion

The lexicon of this broad field appears to have changed in recent times, with the word "diversity" being replaced with the term "inclusion". Organisations can no longer ignore the fact that diversity management has become a critical factor in maintaining marketplace competitiveness and managing talent. Some organisations are moving away from the standard focus on "recruitment initiatives, education and training, career development, and mentoring programmes to increase and retain workforce heterogeneity" (Roberson, 2006: 213), and focusing instead on inclusion in the management of diversity.

The concept of inclusion means removing barriers that prevent employees from using their full range of skills and competences at work. According to Roberson (2006: 213), inclusion is defined as "the extent to which individuals can access information and resources, are involved in work groups, and have the ability to influence decision-making processes". For some organisations, a focus on inclusion has resulted in the development of programmes and initiatives that include employee participation, communication strategies and community relations (Roberson, 2006).

According to Coultas, Bedwell, Burke and Salas (2011), the two trends which have emerged to improve the performance of middle- and top-level leaders are *executive coaching and the cultural diversification* of the workplace. Two key questions arise: how do organisational cultural values affect the coaching of these executives and their teams, and what is the cultural adaptability of the coach to the individual coachee, to the team and to the organisation? The literature to date does not reflect these two questions.

Adapting to multicultural diversity

A major challenge for organisations and institutions today is to manage an increasingly diverse workforce. Individuals must learn to adapt to multicultural diversity, and hence to differences in race, ethnicity, gender, sexual identity, education and language – in addition to a fast-paced, continually changing corporate environment. They must also confront power issues within the hierarchical nature of organisational systems, as well as major economic and life transitions in the workplace.

It has become critically important for business coaches to understand the impact of diversity on team performance, cooperation and conflict, particularly as organisations work in team-based, highly competitive environments. Today, many organisations are opting for team coaching as a more effective way to improve team capability and performance while saving on costs. A key question is how diversity within groups can be developed as a "productive asset rather than becoming a source of conflict and prejudice" (Christian et al. 2006: 459).

Diversity research has focused primarily on six attributes: race, age, gender, education, functional background and tenure (Qin, Muenjohn and Chhetri, 2014: 139). Within the social sciences, research has generally focused on issues of race, ethnicity, gender and age. Other writers have interpreted diversity as "demographic diversity" – that is, meaning any individual characteristics such as educational background, personality traits, learning styles, life and work experience. This approach can, however, be used to subvert any meaningful discussion on diversity issues. Some authors have distinguished between "surface-level" and "deep-level" differences (Chatman and Flynn, 2001; Harrison, Price, Gavin and Florey, 2002). Others have emphasised distinctions between "low-visibility" and "high-visibility" diversity variables and either "low job-relatedness" or "high job-relatedness" (Pelled, 1996: 617).

Common diversity attributes

To better understand the effects of diversity on cohesion and group performance, studies have attempted to classify the most common diversity attributes as being

- readily detectable versus less observable;
- surface-level versus deep-level;
- highly job-related versus less job-related;
- task-related versus relations-oriented and
- role-related versus inherent (Christian et al., 2006: 461).

Harrison, Price and Bell (1998) defined diversity along the dimensions of surface-level (demographic) and deep-level (attitudinal) diversity, based on the hypothesis that "as people interact to get to know one another, stereotypes are replaced by more accurate knowledge of each other as individuals" (Lee and Farh, 2004: 140). According to Jarzabkowski and Searle (2004: 405), diversity is important to the strategic capacity of the top team, enhancing its capacity to deal with dynamic and volatile environments and improve corporate performance. Diversity is, however, a complex matter which involves demographic, informational and behavioural differences that may be difficult to manage effectively.

Demographic diversity refers to obvious differences, such as gender, age and race. "The longer a team is together the more members gain familiarity with each other and the less demographic measures indicate true diversity. Over time, differences of race, gender or age become familiar and cease to be remarkable" (Jarzabkowski and Searle, 2004: 400).

Informational diversity is related to the different functional, experiential and educational backgrounds that members bring to a team. This diversity provides information and knowledge upon which the team draws. Diverse industry experience adds to the strategic capacity of the team by broadening the boundaries for envisioning strategic opportunities (Jarzabkowski and Searle, 2004: 402).

Behavioural diversity involves different personality styles within a team (Jarzabkowski and Searle, 2004: 400). Personality is a more robust indicator of difference, and the personality composition of the team will strongly affect the way members work together (Jarzabkowski and Searle, 2004: 403–404) and manage conflict. Important here is that "psychological measures can expose hidden diversity that might affect collective strategic action" (Jarzabkowski and Searle, 2004: 405).

Managing diversity

The term "diversity management" originated in North America, but has slowly taken hold in other regions of the world. Barak (2014: 218) suggests the following definition:

> Diversity management refers to the voluntary organisational actions that are designed to create greater inclusion of employees from various backgrounds into the formal and informal organisational structures through deliberate policies and programmes.

Research over the past 20 years shows mixed results as to how diversity impacts the strategic capacity of a business. A broad conclusion is that

> mixed-composition work groups can improve group performance by providing a wider range of perspectives and a broader skills base – but simultaneously it can be detrimental to group cohesion and performance because the diversity in personal backgrounds has the potential to exert a negative influence.
>
> (Christian et al., 2006: 460)

The two most common theoretical approaches in the diversity management literature are as follows:

- the *information/decision-making perspective*, which proposes that differences within a group's composition should be positively related to group performance, through greater variability in skills, abilities and perspectives; and
- the *social categorisation perspective*, which suggests that work group diversity can be detrimental to satisfaction and performance – as group members will use similarities and differences between themselves to construct significant characteristics for comparison (Christian et al., 2006: 462).

According to Hewlett, Marshall and Sherbin (2013), new research provides compelling evidence that diversity unlocks innovation and drives market growth. The researchers examined two kinds of diversity: inherent and acquired. *Inherent diversity* involves traits people are born with, such as gender, ethnicity and sexual orientation. *Acquired diversity* involves traits gained from experience. Leaders exhibiting at least three inherent and three acquired diversity traits are referred to as having two-dimensional diversity. Their research found that companies with two-dimensional diversity out-innovate and outperform others (Hewlett et al., 2013).

In two-dimensional firms, "outside-the-box" ideas are heard, and employees are 45 per cent likelier to report a growth in market share over the previous year and 70 per cent likelier to report that the firm captured a new market. Without diverse leadership, women staff members are 20 per cent less likely than heterosexual white men to win endorsement for their ideas; people of colour are 24 per cent less likely; and lesbian, gay, bisexual or trans-gender people are 21 per cent less likely. Further, a team with a member who shares a client's ethnicity is 152 per cent likelier than another team to understand that client (Hewlett et al., 2013). This indicates an important conclusion for business coaches – leaders need acquired diversity to establish a culture in which all employees feel free to contribute ideas.

Barak (2014) distinguishes between the "exclusion workplace" and the "inclusive workplace". The exclusion workplace operates within a context that is ethnocentric and focused on specific financial and national interests. In contrast, the inclusive workplace sees value in collaborating across national borders, being pluralistic and identifying global mutual interests. The inclusive workplace encourages and facilitates the inclusion of individual employees who are different from the mainstream at of four levels:

- Level 1 – the workplace values and utilises individual and intergroup differences within its work forces.
- Level 2 – the workplace cooperates with and contributes to its surrounding community.
- Level 3 – the workplace alleviates the needs of disadvantaged groups in its wider national environment.
- Level 4 – the workplace collaborates with individuals, groups and organisations across national and cultural boundaries (Barak, 2014: 306–307).

Conclusion

The importance of coaches understanding diversity and culture, especially for team coaching, cannot be overemphasised. The challenges and opportunities presented by diversity will only increase as the pace of social change and interaction speeds up. Above all, the coach needs to constantly work on their own assumptions and cultural understanding – a lifelong process of learning and empathy.

Note

Elements of this section have been adapted from parts of the following chapter: Stout-Rostron, S. (2017). Culturality in coaching. In Greif, S., Möller, H., and Scholl, W. (eds), *Handbuch Schlüsselkonzepte im Coaching* (*Handbook of Key Concepts in Coaching*), pp. 95–103. Berlin: Springer Verlag.

References

Barak, M.E. (2014). *Managing Diversity: Toward a Globally Inclusive Workplace.* Third Edition. London: Sage.

Chatman, J.A., and Flynn, F.J. (2001). The influence of demographic heterogeneity on the emergence and consequences of co-operative norms in work teams. *Academy of Management Journal*, 44(5):956–974.

Christian, J., Porter, L.W., and Moffitt, G. (2006). Workplace diversity and group relations: An overview. *Group Processes and Intergroup Relations*, 9(4):459–466.

Coultas, C.W., Bedwell, W.L., Burke, C.S., and Salas, E. (2011). Values-sensitive coaching: The DELTA approach to coaching culturally diverse executives. *Consulting Psychology Journal: Practice and Research*, 63:149–161.

Cross, T., Bazron, B., Dennis, K., and Isaacs, M. (1989). *Towards a Culturally Competent System of Care: Volume I*. Washington, DC: CASSP Technical Assistance Center, Georgetown University.

Deal, T.E., and Kennedy, A.A. (2000). *Corporate Cultures: The Rites and Rituals of Corporate Life*. Second Edition. New York, NY: Perseus.

Earley, P.C., and Mosakowski, E. (2004). Cultural intelligence. *Harvard Business Review*, 82(10):1–9.

Egan, M.L., and Bendick, M. (2008). Combining multicultural management and diversity into one course on cultural competence. *Academy of Management Learning and Education*, 7(3):387–393.

Harrison, D.A., Price, K.H., and Bell, M.P. (1998). Beyond relational demography: Time and the effects of surface- and deep-level diversity on work group cohesion. *Academy of Management Journal*, 41(1):96–107.

Harrison, D.A., Price, K.H., Gavin, J.H., and Florey, A. (2002). Time, teams, and task performance: Changing effects of surface- and deep-level diversity on group functioning. *Academy of Management Journal*, 45(5):1029–1045.

Hewlett, S.A., Marshall, M., and Sherbin, L. (2013). How diversity can drive innovation. *Harvard Business Review*, 91(12):30–30.

Hofstede, G. (1980). *Culture's Consequences: International Differences in Work-Related Values*. London: Sage.

Hofstede, G. (2001). *Culture's Consequences: Comparing Values, Behaviours, Institutions, and Organisations across Nations*. Thousand Oaks, CA: Sage.

Jarzabkowski, P., and Searle, R.H. (2004). Harnessing diversity and collective action in the top management team. *Long Range Planning*, 37:399–419.

Javidan, M., and House, R.J. (2001). Cultural acumen for the global manager: Lessons from Project GLOBE. *Organisational Dynamics*, 29(4):289–305.

Kahn, M.S. (2014). *Coaching on the Axis: Working with Complexity in Business and Executive Coaching*. International Edition. London: Karnac.

Lee, C., and Farh, J.-L. (2004). Joint effects of group efficacy and gender diversity on group cohesion and performance. *Applied Psychology: An International Review*, 53(1):136–154.

Matsumoto, D. (1996). *Culture and Psychology*. Pacific Grove, CA: Brooks/Cole.

Pelled, L.H. (1996). Demographic diversity, conflict, and work group outcomes: An intervening process theory. *Organisation Science*, 7(6):615–631.

Qin, J., Muenjohn, N., and Chhetri, P. (2014). A review of diversity conceptualisations: Variety, trends, and a framework. *Human Resource Development Review*, 13(2):133–157.

Robbins, S.P. (2001). *Organisational Behaviour*. Englewood Cliffs, NJ: Prentice-Hall.

Roberson, Q.M. (2006). Disentangling the meanings of diversity and inclusion in organisations. *Group and Organisation Management*, 31(2):212–236.

Schein, E.H. (2004). *Organisational Culture and Leadership*. Third Edition. San Francisco, CA: Jossey-Bass.

Schein, E.H. (2010). *Organisational Culture and Leadership*. Fourth Edition. San Francisco, CA: Jossey-Bass.

Schneier, C.J. (1998). *Establishing Dimensions of South African Ethnicity*. Unpublished Masters dissertation. Johannesburg: University of the Witwatersrand.

Spencer-Oatey, H. (2008). *Culturally Speaking: Culture, Communication and Politeness Theory*. Second Edition. London: Continuum.

6 The case for Ubuntu Coaching

Working with an African coaching meta-model that strengthens human connection in a fast-changing VUCA world

Dumisani Magadlela

Introduction

Ubuntu is an ancient African word meaning "humaneness". It also means "I am what I am because of who we all are". VUCA is an acronym used to describe recent business environments and economic contexts that are characterised by **v**olatility, **u**ncertainty, **c**omplexity and **a**mbiguity (or **a**gility).

This chapter presents an introduction to the concept of Ubuntu Coaching as it has been developed in selected organisational contexts. The chapter describes the theoretical foundations of Ubuntu and the meaning of the concept of Ubuntu Coaching, and presents selected examples of the application of the concept in practice. The chapter also touches on the reasons why this approach to human relationships within organisations is needed more than ever before in the fields of coaching skills, leadership development, human development, talent management and organisational culture change.

Understanding our African business and coaching context

Africa's greatest resource is not the land or minerals for which the continent is known. It is Africa's massive youth bulge that represents the continent's most precious resource (Magadlela, 2016). The African continent has experienced massive resource exploitation for centuries (Mignolo, 2011). There is clear evidence that African leaders in both business and politics have colluded with international business to exploit African countries (Clarke, 2013; Games, 2012). However, this chapter, instead, is about tapping into the ancient wisdom of human relationships and interconnections that remain common within and among many African communities.

My premise for what follows is as follows:

> …it is increasingly evident that we live in a deeply interconnected world… Never before has it become more urgent for us to choose leaders, and to ourselves become leaders, who possess greater awareness and humanity. In this context, Africa has a vital role to play.
>
> (Nussbaum, Palsule and Mkhize, 2010: xxii)

This is a call for global leaders in business and in society to recognise the role African humanistic values can play in transforming the way we do business today. In the same spirit, one of South Africa's iconic freedom fighters, Steve Biko, argued that

> The [current] great powers of the world may have done wonders in giving the world an industrial and military look… [T]he greatest contribution still has to come from Africa – giving the world a more human[e] face.
>
> (Steve Biko, 1978: 51)

Current coach training, leadership skills and talent development programmes in business schools around the world are slowly shifting towards paying greater attention to employee engagement across organisational levels, greater connection with communities and the client base that the business serves. Africa can lead this paradigm shift in doing business differently with the African value systems that already encourage greater human connection.

Since 2000, Africa has been one of the fastest-growing regions in the world. Recent estimates in this African VUCA world suggest that up to 30 per cent of the African population is now earning between US$2 and US$20 per day (Games, 2012). Still, among the continent's lingering challenges are the labour, talent and skills deficits. While technical skills are growing, and being exported disproportionately to what is needed locally, there is a growing urgency to develop coaching and leadership skills that resonate with the local labour force. One of the most common relationship advice tips given to foreign investors and business associates is to "build strong relationships with Africans in the markets in which you operate" (Games, 2012: 13).

A key issue discussed here is understanding coaching in the African workplace beyond demographic dynamics. Leading African economic growth and development role-players, such as the

African Development Bank, the Economic Commission for Africa, the African Union Commission, the United Nations Population Fund and the World Bank, have all indicated that by 2040–2050, Africa will have the largest workforce on earth, exceeding China and India (African Development Bank, 2014).

With Africa's fast-growing population, the need to equip leaders in business, government and civil society, with relevant and "relatable" coaching skills, takes on a more important role beyond technical expertise. Africa is the next frontier for coaching. It has been said that "Africa is not for sissies". This is because doing business in Africa requires a higher level of tough-mindedness.

Coaches operating across Africa would do well to explore the best approaches to impact coaching clients. Coaching is still relatively new for many African businesses. Ubuntu is a concept well known to many Africans. It is referred to as an integral part of leaders' moral compass across different African communities and countries (Khoza, 2011; Mbigi, 2005). An integration of Ubuntu and coaching in the form of the practice of Ubuntu Coaching is a logical step in helping more people access the known benefits of coaching as a professional service.

Coaches working with African professionals must stay in touch with the economic and social changes taking place across African workplaces. In his book *Ubuntu: Shaping the Current Workplace with (African) Wisdom*, Vuyisile Msila (2015) argues that Ubuntu is needed in many current toxic workplaces to infuse positive energy into the organisation and to revitalise teams.

Msila contends that although Ubuntu is not a panacea or silver bullet for all current workplace challenges, it can certainly be useful in helping to build team engagement and promote positive performance. When business leaders regard employees within their organisations as integral parts of an intricately connected system, they have a chance to create positive vibes across the business and remove the "us-and-them" dynamic. This is because, as Msila emphasises, Ubuntu is "grounded in the notion that life is a web of interconnectedness" (Msila, 2015: 5).

It is important that as coaches we fully understand that we are part of constantly changing systems. We are change agents ourselves, and we are also thinking partners for the next generation of global leaders who have the capacity to impact the rest of the world with their "way of being". If these "ways of being" are informed by Ubuntu values of "I am because we are", these leaders can become powerful paradigm shifters.

There is a real chance that Ubuntu Coaching will assist emerging global leaders to focus less on the individual benefit from their leadership, and more on the collective value from their practices. This can also have a major impact on team coaching processes. Ubuntu Coaching means that both private and public sector leaders, together with civil society and/or multi-lateral agency leaders, will become conscious and aware of their capacity to impact their world positively.

A critical aspect in Africa's development is the need to improve the continent's ease of doing business. I believe that Ubuntu, especially as a way of being, and as a way of life that informs our interrelationships in business, is essential to enhance individual and team performance within organisations. Using Ubuntu Coaching at individual, team and organisational levels will help towards improving ways of relating across partners and business stakeholders (Kgomoeswana, 2014: 5).

What is Ubuntu philosophy?

> Ubuntu is best understood experientially.
>
> (Magadlela, 2008: 1)

In many African communities, personal integrity and leadership identity are strongly linked to the practice and ways of Ubuntu. Ubuntu means *humaneness*. Ubuntu is described as recognising and acknowledging that we exist in community and in belonging. It is essentially a relational concept that governs human relationships in communities and within organisations.

The values of Ubuntu are across different parts of the African continent and are described in more or less the same way. Humaneness in Southern Africa is described as *ubuntu*, *botho*, *bantu*, *uhnu*, *chivanhu*, *avandu*, *ubunye* and *isintu*. It has also been described as *ujamaa*, *watu* and *umoja* in East Africa. The same values and characteristics have been described as *ngumtu*, *kubuntu* or *edubuntu* in Central Africa, and as *amani*, *ogbara*, *ise* and *ika* in West Africa (Vilakati, 2016: 482).

Vilakati argues that the concepts describing Ubuntu in the above paragraph represent "the unifying philosophical, anthropological, socio-cultural [and organisational] premise for African thinking about human identity, consciousness, and relational ways of thinking, being and connecting with others..." (Vilakati, 2016: 482). Human connection and humaneness is a deeply felt and experienced part of African values systems.

In many African contexts and situations, these values, attitudes and ways of being have been severely eroded if not completely eradicated by the importation of other ways. It is important for organisations and businesses operating in Africa to understand that

> ...at the foundation of...African human consciousness is the primacy of the development of strong and effective individuals and family. Families and communities [and organisations] can only be as strong as the individuals in them.
>
> (Vilakati, 2016: 483)

These ways and values are found in abundance across different parts of the continent in the form of humaneness, hospitality, sharing, caring, interdependence, belonging, harmony, respect, empathy, cooperation, responsiveness, accountability, compassion, solidarity, humility, connectedness, generosity, social awareness, reciprocity and a host of other virtues that give meaning to one's existence in relation to others (Vilakati, 2016).

This chapter does not go into detail about the historical origins or ontology of Ubuntu or its application in coaching engagements as Ubuntu Coaching. The historical grounding of the philosophy of Ubuntu has been presented in publications by Mbigi (2005), Bhengu (2006), Bhengu (2011) and Khoza (2011).

Ubuntu is an ancient African (Nguni) word meaning "humaneness". The term Ubuntu implies "I am because you are, and you are because we are". It has also been described as meaning "I am who or what I am because of who and what we all are". In other words, it is our human interconnectedness that creates, enables and gives meaning to our interactions and relationships. The broader meaning of this old worldview is drawn from the belief that all human beings have an inherent capacity to connect with their fellow human beings.

Ubuntu has been described as "both a philosophy of life and a worldview" (Khoza, 2006). Khoza describes Ubuntu as

> ...a comprehensive mode through which reality is constructed and shared. The philosophy has multiple dimensions encompassing the moral, philosophical, rational psychological and social. Ubuntu is characterised by such values as caring, reciprocity, sharing, compassion, hospitality, cohabitation, cooperation and tolerance.
>
> (Khoza, 2006: xxii)

One of my favourite Ubuntu descriptions or statements is the one given by our beloved Archbishop Emeritus of Cape Town, Desmond Tutu. He said,

> Africans have a thing called Ubuntu. It is about the essence of being human. It is part of the gift that Africa is going to give to the world. It embraces hospitality, caring about others, being willing to go the extra mile for the sake of another. We believe that a person is a person through other persons; that my humanity is caught up and bound up in yours. When I dehumanise you, I inexorably dehumanise myself. The solitary human being is a contradiction in terms, and therefore you seek to work for the common good because your humanity comes into its own in community, in belonging.
>
> (Tutu, 1995; quoted in Mbigi, 2005: 67)

One of the main challenges in explaining Ubuntu to others who have not had experiential exposure to it is that it comes across as abstract and intangible. This is a regular challenge in undocumented knowledge systems such as Africa's oral history. Knowledge and skills are not codified and explicit, but are uncodified and implicit (Mbigi, 2005).

Ubuntu can be found in almost every African community south of the Sahara. In Nguni languages (found mostly in Southern Africa), Ubuntu is *Umuntu ngumuntu ngabantu*, which literally means "A person is a person through other people". In Kenya, the Kikuyu refer to the concept of Ubuntu as *Umundu nimudu niunde wa andu*. In Zimbabwe, the Shona refer to Ubuntu as *Munhu pamusana pevanhu* (Boon, 2007: 26). These different descriptions of Ubuntu define good human relations as being anchored in service to others.

Mbigi (2005) says that writing about these knowledge systems and ways of being such as Ubuntu will help African wisdom and knowledge become universal. The late former president of South Africa, Nelson Mandela, in his foreword to Reuel Khoza's (2006) book *Let Africa Lead*, suggests that Ubuntu is a vital instrument to "bridge the gaps between people in the workplace, stakeholders within and outside the enterprise and business and the broader society in which they operate" (Mandela, 2006: xxv).

The premise for Ubuntu is collective engagement and consciousness. Bhengu presents this very powerfully when he states that

> Africa believes strongly in the framework of…spirit, soul and body, since the triad involves a synthesis of the three aspects of human social relations: the somatic, pneumatic and psychic – or

> body, mind and spirit. We term this the triad of human consciousness. The Western ideology of capitalism denies Africa all this. It oppresses all the aspects of social relations into non-existence and oblivion, and the challenge is to reverse it.
>
> (Bhengu, 2011: 29)

Leadership practices and values that are imbued with the spirit of Ubuntu can be described as transformational or servant leadership. Msila argues that leaders with Ubuntu are transformational leaders, and they and their organisations have the following characteristics:

- They are driven by success vision.
- They are accommodating and thoughtful of others.
- They are able to think and work in teams, and can be independent and self-driven.
- They value the role of community.
- They are not afraid of criticism, but value being shown the right direction (Msila, 2015: 103).

Coaches that are trained in the Ubuntu Coaching approach or framework use their new lenses to see the human interconnections that are present in just about every human interaction. The demographic conundrum of mixed generations in the VUCA world requires more accepting and accommodating coaching approaches such as Ubuntu Coaching. Transactional models, or those that cater mainly for individual performance above collective accountability, start from a weak point of giving less credence to the role of the workplace community.

Ubuntu Coaching clearly calls for organisational leaders to see the other in the system. When the leaders start from a premise of respect for others (seeing them, as in the Nguni greeting "I see you"), there is greater scope and room for employee engagement and team collaboration. This is a useful premise for Ubuntu Coaching as presented in the next session below.

Conceptualising Ubuntu Coaching

Ubuntu Coaching refers to the active application of Ubuntu principles and values in the practice of the professional field of executive and leadership coaching. This can be applied in all modalities of human development such as business coaching, performance coaching, workplace mentoring, executive development and talent management. There is a strong case to be made that

> Fully integrating [the] fundamental principles of African human consciousness into the ethos of effective business team leadership has not been done sufficiently.
>
> (Vilakati, 2016: 483)

There is a long way to go before these integrating values and ways of being or relating to others are incorporated into business practice. At the centre of the application of Ubuntu-based practices in the practice of coaching is the recognition of Ubuntu's ethos of what has been termed "the African concept of consultative dialogue", which is inherently "consensus-building" (Vilakati, 2016: 483). There is a massive scope for forward-thinking businesses to incorporate these old African principles into their business practices. Ubuntu Coaching is one way of bringing them into the boardroom.

Ubuntu means that what I am is a result of who we are as relational human beings. In other words, what I am and what I do impacts you and the next person. In turn, what you do has implications for me and others too.

We cannot afford to continue thinking, planning and acting, in mini-silos called national interests, or in shallow business interests. We must all think and act systemically with the global perspective in mind. In its relationship with business, Mandela describes Ubuntu as follows:

> Humaneness does not weaken business. It strengthens it. It cements the relationships upon which teamwork and innovation must rest. It builds trust among employees, customers, and communities. Both teamwork and trust are seen as vital components of world-class enterprises today.
>
> (Mandela, 2006: xxiv)

Ubuntu Coaching is predicated on this core value system of humaneness and interrelationships. It is inherently a systems-based meta-model of coaching that both demands and enables leaders to "see systems" in their outlook on business and in their leadership, starting with close personal relationships and extending out to the community to national and global interests.

Ubuntu is essentially the bedrock of transformational leadership in the context of our fast-changing VUCA business world. It behoves us to shift from the individual focus of most dated western individualistic business ideologies, and adopt shared worldviews that place greater value on the collective, the community, the organisation, the environment, than the individual.

In describing the skills that are highly relevant to the coaching world, Stout-Rostron refers to a range of skills that she argues come from psychotherapy. These skills relate directly to the principles and values of Ubuntu and include active listening, empathy, self-awareness, process observation, conflict resolution and learned optimism, among others (Stout-Rostron, 2012: 41). Ubuntu gives us an opportunity to connect to others as we engage and work with them from a stance of non-judgement. Non-judgement is an integral skill to effective coaching.

One of the important aspects of Ubuntu Coaching is how leaders conduct meetings. In Ubuntu-led meetings, the leader uses tried and tested Ubuntu "guidelines" for conducting meetings in the *umhlangano* (meeting in isiZulu) or in *inkundla* (or place of meeting). In Sesotho (Lesotho) or Setswana (Botswana), the common term for meetings is called *lekgotla* (place of meeting) (De Liefde, 2007). These old traditional concepts are similar to what Nancy Kline describes as the Thinking Environment® in her seminal work *Time to Think* (Kline, 1999).

Ubuntu Coaching lends itself directly to this perspective especially because of the relational nature of human connection in workplaces. Toxic workplaces are characterised by poor human relationships. Ubuntu is inherently about valuing relationships within the systems that we work or operate in as coaches and coaching clients. Ubuntu Coaching enhances the intentional development or conscious growing of mutually supportive workplace relationships.

Coming home to our humaneness

Coaching is powerfully transformational in its impact. Transformational coaching practices demand that the coach be fluid, agile and especially *responsive* to the changes taking place around them. Being responsive requires that as coaches we must be in touch with our social, cultural and business context (or operating environment).

The emergence of coaching as a mainstream part of human capital, talent management, executive development and general business leadership practices is testimony to the value of this relatively young profession. One of the blind sides of coaching is the rather limited attention to the cultural context where coaches practise their craft. This is especially true in dynamic and fast-changing socio-economic environments such as coaching's next frontier, the African continent and its burgeoning youth population that is connected to mobile technology and is increasingly innovative. This attention to the principles, practice and philosophy of Ubuntu is a direct response to the need to address this issue in, for example, the African context.

The emerging African coaching framework encapsulated in Ubuntu Coaching is gaining traction among coaching practitioners. It is being increasingly used by leadership skills development trainers and coach training institutions in South Africa and other parts of the African continent.

Ubuntu Coaching is about helping us all remember our *inherent human interconnectedness*. It is meant to trigger our natural capacity to tune-in to each other in a caring and less aggressive or less self-serving and selfish ways. This is already happening in communities where people choose to care for each other who have very little to share among themselves while billions of dollars' worth of food, for example, is thrown away as waste across the so-called rich world, and sometimes in pockets of wealth in some of the poorest countries in the world.

Ubuntu Coaching as a systems meta-model

Nelson Mandela is one of the legends of Ubuntu leadership. In his foreword to a book by Reuel Khoza, Mandela describes Ubuntu's relevance in modern business as follows:

> Ubuntu in business can help bridge gaps between people in the workplace, stakeholders within and outside the enterprise, [between] businesses and the broader society in which they operate. As a uniquely African moral philosophy, Ubuntu belongs in business life on this continent, just as it does in our political and social lives. Ubuntu promotes cohabitation: the tolerance and acceptance of all races and creeds in the human household. Every household has an economy and there is the potential for conflict in every household. Ubuntu reminds people in the household that they are all part of the greater human family and that all depend on each other. It promotes peace and understanding.
>
> (Mandela, 2006: xxv–xxvi)

In a similar stance that enhances mutually supportive human relationships, Bhengu (2011) suggests that modern business and global commerce require a new model or way of organisation. Bhengu (2011: 3) calls for the development and adoption of what he calls "African economic humanism".

The premise of this approach to doing business and organising human relationships is that

> (I)t is through the inclusion of African humanistic values, such as being concerned with the needs of others, being sensitive to others'

> religious and cultural beliefs and a total commitment to the well-being of all, that humane economic relations will be enabled.
>
> (Bhengu, 2011: 175)

By its very nature, coaching is a service to both the individual and the collective. In supporting the individual professional, manager, executive or C-suite organisational leader, coaching inevitably serves the greater good through helping enhance the best of each role-player along the broader human network or system. Stout-Rostron argues that as coaches we must be constantly aware of our context and notice our client system's dominant culture (individualistic, materialistic, collective or humanistic). She encourages coaches to be self-aware in their coaching practice by asking questions such as whether the client is individualistic or collectivistic (Stout-Rostron, 2012: 172).

In terms of the coaching process and its impact on the individual client or coachee, most coaches understand that their coaching competencies require that they track the work of the client across various stages of shifts from the current state to the desired state. Stout-Rostron maintains that the coachee's work tends to start with "growing self-awareness, increased emotional maturity and improved interpersonal skills and competence" (Stout-Rostron, 2012: 47).

In order to not only notice but also accurately track the progress that the client is making, the coach must start from the coaching stance of "positive regard". This means that the coach must conduct themselves with genuine empathy at all times. These are the qualities that Rogers (1961: 47–49), cited in Stout-Rostron (2012: 49), describes as essential characteristics of an effective and supportive relationship.

In his book *Social Intelligence*, Daniel Goleman suggests that great listening, which is an essential ingredient in effective communication, starts with attunement to the other. Goleman describes attunement as "attention that goes beyond momentary empathy to a full, sustained presence that facilitates rapport" (Goleman, 2006: 86). In the context of Ubuntu and the lekgotla, or Kline's Thinking Environment, the emphasis is on listening attentively, with deep mindfulness and attention to the other's feelings, instead of the selfish gratification of "my need to be heard at all cost".

Ubuntu is essentially the ideal way of promoting harmonious co-existence with fellow beings and with nature. The question then becomes, HOW do we bring this about in our chosen vision of coaching? We bring in Ubuntu into coach training and practice.

My preliminary suggestions on this were that, as coaches working within organisations, we can rally every coach across the world and spread the power and value of Ubuntu Coaching regarding the fast-paced changes of our VUCA world. We can nudge every single leader we coach towards greater connection and engagement with their teams. This would be done by raising all coached leaders' awareness of the inherent human capacity to connect to other humans, other beings and to nature. Nature is all our finite human support system and not an infinite or endless well of natural resources.

With organisations, as coaches, we can impact the world through transforming organisational cultures. Recently, I used Ubuntu Coaching in the introduction and development of a new organisational culture for one of my clients with amazingly positive results especially in employee engagement and connection across structural levels and roles and across functions.

The link between Ubuntu Coaching and Gestalt Organisational Development

Gestalt is a psychological term that "loosely translated, means 'unified whole'. The word also refers to the configuration of a set of elements perceived as whole" (Rainey and Hanafin, 2018: 1). The following are among the leading Gestalt Organisational Development principles that guide Gestalt interveners when working with organisations. Gestalt coaches and practitioners believe the following:

- growth and development are options of the client, not the intervener (or coach);
- change can occur simply by heightening awareness;
- the task of the intervener (or coach) is to help the client become more aware of what helps and hinders growth and development;
- resistance is a healthy, positive, creative force and
- the group is the primary unit of intervention in Gestalt Organisational Development, with interventions at other levels that support and expand work at group level (Rainey and Hanafin, 2018: 11).

The link between Gestalt Organisational Development and Ubuntu Coaching is in the recognition of the role of the collective (and not the individual) in catalysing change. There is a greater momentum in the group to drive and effect system-wide change. Gestalt Organisational Development practitioners are trained in mastering how to intervene at all levels of an organisational system: individual, pairs (dyads), groups and large systems.

Gestalt Organisational Development focuses on developing interveners' skills to use self (their presence) in raising client system awareness. The intervener (or coach) learns how to pick up figures that emerge from the intervention and raise the client's awareness to them. The awareness is what the client needs to make shifts in the system. Ubuntu Coaching works in the same way in its specific focus on the group or broader system's awareness of the need to make shifts. Awareness is the most powerful catalyst for change in all levels of the system. Like Ubuntu Coaching, Gestalt Organisational Development is systemic.

Practical applications of Ubuntu Coaching

The Ubuntu Team Coaching lekgotla Meeting

Ubuntu is especially powerful when human beings need to make decisions that have a social, group, team, organisational, even international impact. The lekgotla is a fluid collective engagement and a decision-making process where everyone gets a chance to air their views and be listened to by the collective.

There are various types of lekgotla processes. The one described below is for managing team meetings, and is strikingly similar to Nancy Kline's Thinking Environment (Kline, 1999) or the American Talking Stick method. This is an ancient process for engagement in many societies around the world.

The Ubuntu Team Coaching lekgotla Seven-Step Process© is given as follows:

1 The group elects one of them to be the session's Chief.
2 The Chief outlines the topic or main issue for discussion and/or decision-making.
3 Everyone in the session takes turns to share his or her views on the selected topic.
4 When all have spoken, the Chief summarises key issues (common understanding).
5 The Chief puts the final matter(s) to the collective vote: and makes a recommendation.
6 The Chief then thanks everyone, wraps up the meeting or moves to the next issue.
7 Within organisations, the group can now select another Chief for the next topic.

Note to facilitator

These steps are flexible and can vary, or be adapted, depending on the interests of the group, or on the organisation's dominant culture. They do not have to be seven. They can be less or more depending on the context. In an organisation without a strong Coaching Culture, or with significantly low levels of employee engagement, this process can help build greater engagement and help break down silos. This way of managing meetings can also support teams to engage with each other openly and safely across the organisation's structures or levels.

Ubuntu "notice and connect" exercise

As we go about our everyday business, we encounter fellow beings on their own business. In some cultures, making contact and greeting everyone you meet is standard practice. In isiZulu (the most commonly spoken local language in Southern Africa), when we greet we say *Sawubona*, which literally translates as "I see you". In other cultures, people pass each other daily with no need, nor expectation, to greet or acknowledge the other at all. In some eastern cultures (e.g. Japan), people nod, or bow, to acknowledge or greet each other.

This is important whether we are attending a meeting, at the office water cooler, walking the workplace corridors, in the elevator, or in open public spaces, such as the mall, at the gas station, or taking a walk alongside a road, or on a beach. It is important to *notice*. Then, after noticing, make a considered effort to *connect* to or with whoever you notice might be ready or willing to connect. We are inherently connecting human beings, and when we make even a little effort to connect to/with others, however different from us they seem externally, we become more self-aware and more aware of others.

Note to facilitator

This exercise is most effective when conducted over a period of eight hours (which is a normal business or working day). Keep track of how many people you actually make genuine connection with, and notice whether there are patterns in who you find easy to approach. This exercise has been used with trainee coaches, and with youth leaders, to help them refine their engagement technique for establishing authentic connection.

The Ubuntu Team Coaching Circle

This exercise is often used with groups of officials or employees within an organisation who work together and are familiar with each other. It combines aspects of the lekgotla process for managing meetings, and elements of Gestalt Coaching or awareness (such as the "use of self"). The exercise helps build or strengthen high-performing teams within organisations. The Ubuntu Coaching Circles can include team member numbers from 5 to 15 members. Ideally, it is better to keep the numbers relatively small (below 15), to ensure that within the given time (two to three hours), every member in the circle gets to fully express themselves and/or inquire with circle members on any issues of common interest that they feel strongly about. The "circle" is derived from the sitting arrangement, which is a semicircle or a full circle without tables.

1 Schedule a Circle meeting weeks ahead: participants must know ahead of time.
2 Prepare the Circle's list of discussion issues (agenda) and share with all participants.
3 Ideally, select the facilitator before each Circle session (known to all participants).
4 Prepare the room to allow a circular seating arrangement with no tables.
5 Participants all check in individually. Facilitator leads the check-in and models it.
6 Facilitator ensures that everyone takes turns to speak up.
7 All participants express how the agenda and engagement supports their collective goals.
8 Facilitator connects the themes and key issues raised, and sums up the discussion.
9 Participants all check out with something that connects their group/team in the spirit of Ubuntu, and what strengthens their Circle.

Conclusion

Coaching is fast becoming one of the most powerful service professions in modern workplaces. Ubuntu Coaching is still new. As an emerging African coaching perspective in what is essentially a Western-developed coaching profession, Ubuntu Coaching adds to the growing body of knowledge in our profession. The Ubuntu Coaching framework, while still needing further refinement, offers a fresh approach that many African coaches and coaching clients can relate to.

The juxtaposing of the individual versus the collective is a well-known sociological and psychological conundrum that will remain with us for a while to come. African coaches, and global coaching practitioners working in this exciting frontier, will serve themselves better by paying attention to this useful tool to enhance human relationships within businesses and in society. Ubuntu Coaching is a perspective that the profession cannot ignore. It governs human relationships be they formal or informal across the African business landscape.

References

African Development Bank. (2014). *The Bank's Human Capital Strategy for Africa (2014–2018)*. Abidjan: Human Development Department (OSHD), African Development Bank.

Bhengu, M.J. (2006). *Ubuntu: The Global Philosophy for Humankind*. Cape Town: Lotsha.

Bhengu, M.J. (2011). *African Economic Humanism: The Rise of an African Economic Philosophy*. London: Gower.

Biko, S.B. (1978). *Steve Biko: I Write What I Like: A Selection of His Writings*. Edited by Aelred Stubbs. London: Heinemann.

Boon, M. (2007). *The African Way: The Power of Interactive Leadership*. Cape Town: Zebra.

Clarke, D. (2013). *Africa's Future: Darkness to Destiny: How the Past Is Shaping Africa's Economic Evolution*. London: Profile.

Games, D. (2012). *Business In Africa: Corporate Insights*. Johannesburg: Penguin.

Goleman, D. (2006). *Social Intelligence: The New Science of Human Relationships*. New York, NY: Bantam Dell.

Kgomoeswana, V. (2014). *Africa Is Open for Business: Ten Years of Game-Changing Headlines*. Johannesburg: Macmillan.

Khoza, R.J. (2006). *Let Africa Lead: African Transformational Leadership for 21st Century Business*. Johannesburg: Vezubuntu.

Khoza, R.J. (2011). *Attuned Leadership: African Humanism as Compass*. Johannesburg: Penguin.

Kline, N. (1999). *Time to Think: Listening to Ignite the Human Mind*. London: Cassell Illustrated.

Magadlela, D. (2008). *(Mis)understanding ubuntu: A reply*. Thoughtleader.co.za blog posting 16 March 2008. URL: thoughtleader.co.za/dumisanimagadlela/2008/03/16/mis-understanding-ubuntu-a-reply/.

Magadlela, D. (2016). *Can You Teach a Lion to Roar? Selected African Skills Development and Capacity Building Perspectives: Breaking Down Old Paradigms and Creating New Opportunities*. Working Paper No. 16–03. Kunitachi, Tokyo: Institute of Innovation Research, Hitotsubashi University.

Mandela, N.R. (2006). Foreword. In Khoza, R.J. (ed.), *Let Africa Lead: African Transformational Leadership for 21st Century Business*, pp. xxiv–xxxiii. Johannesburg: Vezubuntu.

Mbigi, L. (2005). *The Spirit of African Leadership*. Johannesburg: Knowres.

Mignolo, W.D. (2011). *The Darker Side of Western Modernity: Global Futures, Decolonial Options*. Durham, NC: Duke University Press.

Msila, V. (2015). *Ubuntu: Shaping the Current Workplace with (African) Wisdom*. Johannesburg: Knowres.

Nussbaum, B., Palsule, S., and Mkhize, V. (2010). *Personal Growth African Style*. Johannesburg: Penguin.

Rainey, M.A., and Hanafin, J. (2018). *iGold Journal: Alumni Edition*. Cape Town: GestaltOD Partners.

Rogers, C.R. (1961). *On Becoming a Person: A Therapist's View of Psychotherapy*. London: Constable and Robinson.

Stout-Rostron, S. (2012). *Business Coaching Wisdom and Practice. Unlocking the Secrets of Business Coaching*. Second Edition. Johannesburg: Knowres.

Tutu, D. (1995). Nothing short of a miracle. In Thick, C. (ed.), *The Right to Hope: Global Problems, Global Visions: Creative Responses to Our World in Need*, pp. 1–4. London: Earthscan.

Vilakati, V. (2016). African leadership. In Veldsman, T.H., and Johnson, A.J. (eds), *Leadership: Perspectives from the Frontline*, pp. 477–493. Johannesburg: Knowres.

7 Relationship Systems Coaching

Creina Schneier and Anne Rød

Introduction

In this chapter, we share our belief that Relationship Systems Coaching (RSC) is crucial in working with teams in the context of diversity and the fast-paced change in the organisational workplace today. We briefly describe the origins of RSC and Relationship Systems Intelligence™ (a key competence at the core of RSC enabling us to work effectively with human relationship systems). We showcase tools that can be used to apply the principles, to move a team system forward towards achieving greater levels of alignment, collaboration and performance. Finally, we describe the three-phased structure that guides any RSC engagement towards effectively achieving results and sustainable success in teams and organisations.

Why Relationship Systems Coaching?

Human relationship systems form the fabric of every aspect of human society, including organisational work spaces. Generating awareness of a system as a whole tapestry, including the distinctive threads within it, and building capacity to weave these optimally for the benefit of the entire tapestry, is the essence of RSC.

We constantly impact on, and are impacted upon by others, and by the networks of relationships that we are part of. We develop skills to interact with others – some successful, others less so; some conscious, others less so. By becoming more aware of these interactions, of what works and what doesn't, we can become more conscious and intentional in how we engage with others, in order to work toward a more meaningful and beneficial outcome for all of those involved (Rød and Fridjhon, 2016).

The focus of this chapter is a work team, or team system, an interdependent group of individuals interlinked through a shared purpose. This could be a group who work together physically or virtually on a regular basis, a project team, senior leadership team or an executive board.

Most work teams operate today in contexts of continuous change, in which uncertainty, ambiguity and complexity prevail. Increased globalisation, rapidly evolving technologies, unpredictable politics and increasingly scarce resources are but a few sources of escalating complexity within organisational environments, driving the need for continuous individual and organisational learning (Ness, 2014). Workplaces are also characterised by deepening diversity, particularly cultural and generational. For the first time in history, five distinct generations, each with their own tendencies and typical "identity markers", occupy work spaces simultaneously (Pollak, 2017). As a result, more traditional leadership styles of "command and control" do not work. Leaders are constantly challenged to discover new, more effective inclusive leadership processes that will enable them to navigate this context.

Teams navigating workspaces consequently need a different set of skills, and competencies in order to enhance positivity in their members across all generations and cultures, to unleash discretionary effort and to optimise their effectiveness. RSC works with leaders and teams to achieve these outcomes.

A new type of intelligence

Working from a relationship systems perspective involves redirecting focus from the individuals in the team to the team system itself. This implies a shift in awareness from "I" to "we" and from "me" to "us", a "completely different way of approaching leadership and team interactions" (Rød and Fridjhon, 2016: xii).

Relationship System Intelligence is the brainchild of Marita Fridjhon and Faith Fuller. It is fostered in many ways, including the Organisation and Relationship Systems Coaching (ORSC™) methodology, offered by CRR Global (Rød and Fridjhon, 2016: xiii). ORSC offers a rich toolbox that can be accessed by both team coaches and leaders to generate innovative responses to the fast pace of change that is the context for many organisations today.

Relationship System Intelligence includes and builds on emotional and social intelligence as these intelligences have been presented and described by Daniel Goleman (1998; 2006). Emotional intelligence is a focus on self and requires self-awareness to understand one's own emotions and experiences. Social intelligence adds the awareness of other people in order to understand and empathise with their emotions and experiences. Relationship System Intelligence includes both. It is an awareness of, and focus on, the relationship system itself, holding the experiences of all the individuals within the system as expressions of that system and possible signposts of that particular system's needs, insights and aspirations.

Relationship System Intelligence is the ability to see and understand each team member's experience as both personal and an expression of the team system (Rød and Fridjhon, 2016: 13). This allows us to engage with a team in a way that fully embraces its diversity and taps into its inherent creativity and wisdom. In turn, this increases awareness, expands possibilities and places the relationship system and its members on a more solid basis for alignment and collaboration to move the team forward.

The three-phased approach

The interactive, overlapping three-phase structure is a guide that ensures more effective and productive interventions by helping a team to recognise where they are in the process and what might be needed next. The three interactive and overlapping phases are as follows: *meet, reveal and understand, align and action* (Rød and Fridjhon, 2016: 47).

1 Meeting up

The initial phase is when team members meet one another – and learn to engage with their team entity. Handy questions in this phase are as follows:

- What attracted you to join this team/organisation, and what keeps you here?
- What is working well for you in your role/team right now?
- What are you most passionate about in your life/work right now?

These questions are all phrased positively, which sets the tone. The answers elicited start to reveal the team to itself, and automatically move the process to the next phase.

A key tool in this phase is working with the team agreement, which sets the standard for their work together while providing a safe container.

2 Revealing and understanding

In this phase, the team's resourcefulness and creativity are mined and harnessed. There may be conflicts and difficulties as new information is revealed, and it is important to work with these as *signals* which indicate what is trying to emerge. Here, it is important to spend time building the collective intelligence in the team to make it easier to move towards alignment in the next phase.

3 Aligning and taking action

This explores possibilities presented by the newfound awareness, how and on the basis of what, the team can align. Alignment is not the same as agreement. Agreement requires a shared opinion or position. Alignment indicates a level of mutual coordination of interest and commitment to achieve a higher goal, the ability to put personal positions aside to serve a common interest (Rød and Fridjhon, 2016: 29). Taking action is a natural step that emerges from the energy created in alignment. Questions that elicit alignment are as follows:

- Given what has been revealed about us, around what can the team align?
- What is at stake if we do not align?
- What needs must be filled for the alignment to take place?

Co-responsibility and co-accountability can be anchored at this point by asking the team to answer which *outer and inner roles* are required to forward the action that will enable the team to fulfil its purpose. Probing for personal commitments reinforces individual and collective accountability to action.

Each one of these phases follows on naturally from the previous one. The time spent on each is dictated by the task at hand. Two essential thrusts underscore each stage: an impetus to build sufficient safety in the team to contain the work (coupled with building accountability at every step), and the continuous co-creation of awareness as the basis for intentional action.

Implementing Relationship Systems Coaching

Before engaging in any type of RSC, we need to create sufficient safety to engage the team. This is done through a team agreement where the team is invited to share expectations and needs, and create agreements to achieve and fulfil these. Central to this is a level of co-responsibility and shared commitment.

Application: team agreement and expectations

Purpose: to create safety and set ground rules for engagement.
Time: 30–60 minutes, depending on the size of and level of trust in, the team.

A simple way of creating a team agreement and expectations is to ask the team:

- What do we expect from this team in the way that we work together?
  For example: We are a team that listens and respects diverse opinions.
- What agreements do we need to make to each other, and our team, if we are to fulfil our expectations?
  For example: When someone speaks we will listen to understand, without interrupting until they have finished.
- How do we act and respond to each other if things become difficult between us?
  For example: We will ensure each voice is heard and trust others' positive intention.

This exercise, although seemingly simple, can take time to complete. It needs to be in place before proceeding with any other of the tools or exercises described in this chapter, as it ensures the necessary safety in the team for RSC to be successful.

Once the team agreement is in place, we can bring focus to the team entity through building Relationship System Intelligence. The relationship system, or "team" or "relationship entity", is a dynamic force that is created between the individuals in the team. Although intangible, we know it is there because we can "feel" it. Focusing on the team entity allows us to access new information that enables the team as a whole to optimise its resources and intelligence (Rød and Fridjhon, 2016: 17).

Each relationship system is unique. What works in one may not work as well in another. As team coach or leader, our work is underpinned by some key ideas. These influence the way we engage, and can be useful in determining which specific tools and skills may best serve the team at any point in time, in order to move forward and deepen understanding. Our capacity to work deeply with these basic concepts develops as we gain experience.

Moving from "I" to "we"

In moving the attention from "I" to "we", we become aware of what is between us and connecting us: that is, the team entity. It is a powerful, blended, living tapestry. A loose weave made up of individual uniquely textured threads, with spaces in between. If one thread is removed and another joins, the picture looks different, the spaces are different. If you were to hone in on any one thread, you would see a partial picture. The complete picture is not available to any one thread alone, but requires a step back – what we call a holonic shift. The idea of a holonic shift suggests that individuals are autonomous units, themselves composed of a myriad of smaller parts while simultaneously comprising a larger whole (Mella, 2009). In a team-coaching setting, this idea is used to access new information and wisdom that lie within all of the interactions and spaces in between the threads that create the whole tapestry that is the team entity.

The more we point team members' attention to the team's collective aspirations, needs and agenda, the more easily they can access the wisdom and insights of their team entity. This is the practical shifting from "I" to "we" (Rød and Fridjhon, 2016).

Application: accessing the voice of the team

Purpose: to tap into the collective intelligence of the team entity.
Time: 30–60 minutes, depending on the size of the team and the number of questions.

There are questions we ask to help team members access the wisdom of their team entity, such as the following:

- What does the team need now?
- If the organisation or team had a voice and could give advice, what would that be?
- What does the organisation or team need next with regard to an outcome on this issue?

We frequently invite the team entity to express its voice. We do this by bringing in the "team entity chair" and inviting each team member to shift from "I" to "we". We place the chair in a circle of all team member chairs. We mark it with the team's or organisation's name depending on the desired focus. The physical and visual impact of the "team entity chair" is important. Then, we craft questions that are relevant to the matter at hand. For example, if the team is developing a new strategy, questions might include the following:

- What would serve us best right now?
- Where do we need to have our focus?
- What are we not yet aware of?

First, we go around the circle, hearing each team member's response to a particular question. This gives everyone an opportunity to express his/her thoughts without interruption. Secondly, once everybody has spoken, there is an invitation to each team member to sit in the "team entity chair" and experience the questions from the team or the organisation's perspective. Team members are invited to be open to any insights that might come from the "team entity chair" – and it is clear when the person occupying the chair speaks from their individual perspective or that of the team. This offers new insights, ideas and solutions, and team members often remark with surprise on the positive impact of these. We have found that when a team has once gone through this process, they frequently take the "team entity chair", literally or figuratively, into team meetings. The "team entity chair" proves useful in provoking thinking that moves beyond the needs of the "I", encouraging a shift to "we".

Hearing all the voices

To get the most comprehensive picture possible, the most accurate expression of the reality experienced by that relationship system at that point in time, we must hear all the voices, even the less popular ones. Although all voices are not equal in status or importance in a given situation, the more voices we hear, the more information will be available to the team, both in depth and breadth. Sometimes, a leader hears only voices that agree with their own view. If disagreeing voices are not heard, and silence is taken as acceptance of what is being discussed, the potency of the collective wisdom is diminished.

We each own part of the truth as no one is able to see whole picture. We have a tendency to project our partial experiences as the whole truth, ignoring others' partial experiences. This amplifies the importance of hearing all the voices in systems work.

When sufficient safety is created, to welcome all the voices without recrimination, the team's collective intelligence can be expressed as a sum greater than the addition of each individual member, that is, 1 + 1 = 3. A core skill underlying this principle of hearing all the voices (and in building Relationship Systems Intelligence) is listening with attention. When we listen with attention, we work with three domains of attention (Kline, 1999; Whitworth, Kimsey-House, Kimsey-House and Sandahl, 2007). In order for this attention to facilitate genuine listening to understand and to create a sense of safety which conveys an authentic sense of legitimacy to all voices, it is important to be aware of all three domains of attention simultaneously.

Receiving from and influencing the system: three domains of attention

The first domain of attention is "internal listening". We spend most of our time in this domain when we listen to the voice inside our own heads: the consistent flow of automatic thoughts, judgements and comparisons. We are in this domain when we plan our response to what is being said, and when we listen for the first possible gap in order to interject our own thoughts or questions at the expense of listening to understand. Interrupting gives an implicit message that "What I have to say is more important than what you were saying". It undermines the legitimacy of the other person's voice. It is crucial to give the person speaking adequate room to finish expressing themselves.

The second domain of attention is "focused" or "active listening". We listen in this way when we give our complete attention to the content of what the other person is saying, and continue listening fully until they have finished, before we ask the next question. The information we receive from the other person informs our next question and paves the way for a generative process and dialogue. Attention in this domain requires setting aside our automatic thoughts, trusting that when the time comes for us to ask a question or add our own thinking, we will be ready. We will know that when it is our turn, we too will be given sufficient room in which to speak without being interrupted. This focused listening conveys that what you have to say is as legitimate as what I have to say, even though it may differ in its content, and emanate from a different level in the organisation's hierarchy.

The third domain of attention is "global" or "environmental listening". It involves being open to information from all of our senses and from outside the team. It includes listening to what is "not being said", and attending to the atmosphere, or "vibe" in the team, which we call the Emotional Field (Rød and Fridjhon, 2016: 31). It requires a holonic shift, a soft focus on individual voices and a sharper focus on the whole system, including energetic information. Global listening is a dynamic and generative process with incoming and outgoing information. Firstly, the incoming information conveys what lies beyond clearly visible, tangible and spoken material. Secondly, the act of paying active (Domain 2) and global (Domain 3) attention itself, directly impacts the atmosphere or "vibe" in the team creating a space that gives room to and acknowledges others, engenders safety, generates new thinking and welcomes all the voices. It is a Metaskill™ that we can intentionally and actively bring to our work.

Application: rounds

Purpose: to hear all the voices.
Time: Each person can be given 60–120 seconds to speak. Time given depends on the size of the team and the number of Rounds.

We use Rounds to hear all the voices in smaller teams and to practise listening in all three domains of attention. Each team member, in turn, addresses a question. The mind thinks better in the presence of a question (Kline, 1999). This is why, in coaching, we pose questions rather than make statements. Whoever is ready to offer their response to the question begins and chooses a direction the Round will follow, either to their immediate left or right. Certainty of direction puts the mind at ease.

Each person has an equal opportunity to respond to the question while other team members listen with *attention*. If anyone is not ready when it is their turn, they say so. The Round continues in its given direction coming back to that person at the end. Each one speaks once before anyone speaks twice, even the leader. Timing each person's contribution in a Round is useful as it assures each speaker of an equal, uninterrupted time. Implementing Rounds in larger groups can be done by dividing the large group into smaller groups and following the same methodology. It would be important then to share some of the thinking from each of the small groups in the plenary to ensure that voices are heard, perspectives covered and insights shared.

The team is resourceful and has the answers

Relationship systems are naturally intelligent, generative and creative. This principle allows us to trust that the fabric of the tapestry that is our relationship system metaphor will hold and adapt, regardless of the pressures it is under, until the end of its natural life cycle. All fabric eventually disintegrates, and all organisational and team systems have a natural life cycle with a beginning, middle and end. By accepting that all systems have a natural life cycle, it becomes easier to let go of one system and allow another to surface (Rød and Fridjhon, 2016: 21). This might mean someone leaving a system, and another joining, or a change in the whole team.

The generative nature of a team system's collective intelligence can be optimised when people listen with attention to understand, invite in all the voices and trust the team entity. We have often observed how an idea or thought from one team member spirals into a lively discussion that creates a vibrant collective energy generating more ideas and insights than any one individual in the team could on their own.

Application: linear constellation

Purpose: hear all the voices, get a picture of the team's response to an issue, tap into collective intelligence.
Time: 60–90 minutes.

We frequently use a linear constellation as a powerful means of hearing all the voices, while visibly and somatically bringing awareness to the team as a system, to the team entity and the collective intelligence that is built. It offers a potent snapshot of where their team system is at any point in time in relation to a specific issue(s), and where each team member is relative to one another. It is crucial to deepen safety by reassuring team members that there are no right or wrong answers and encouraging them to stand at a point that represents their view, not where they believe others would like to see them to stand.

A tape is placed on the floor in a straight line with sheets of paper numbered 1 to 5. We then invite the team to answer each question we ask, by "voting with their feet" and taking a position on the line that best describes their opinion right now. What tends to bring ease is an assurance that they may take a different position on a different day, but for today, where would they stand?

The questions we ask pertain directly to the team we are working with and the issues they are grappling with. In a recent team engagement, an element of the brief was to work with an internationally based team to create more alignment and collaboration. Some questions we asked were as follows:

On a scale from 1 to 5, where 1 is the lowest and 5 the highest:

- How much do you feel like a team?
- How valued do you feel your contribution is to this team?
- How much collaboration do you experience in the team?

In response to each question, team members constellate on the line. We ask them to become aware of how the whole team is constellated. We ask what they notice and what might be positive or challenging in the picture they see. We then poll various positions on the line by asking people at specific positions to describe the experience of being in that position. Finally, we ask what is needed in order for team members to move towards a 5. Examples of these questions might be the following:

- "What would it take for you to be more like a team?"
- "What do you need in order to feel that your contribution is more valued by this team?" or
- "What is needed for you to collaborate more in this team?"

All these questions open up tremendous insights and new ideas about how the team can move forward by dipping into the team's inherent resourcefulness and creativity. We have found that, as with Rounds, teams adopt this tool in meetings. It saves time, provides a whole team picture and raises pertinent questions that lead to focused dialogue and alignment.

Leadership belongs to the team

Given the complexity of the environment, we understand leadership as belonging to the team and being a shared role. If we want to create ownership and engagement in a team, leadership that is "abdicated" to the functional leader is not a feasible approach. Therefore, a leader applying RSC will consciously and intentionally work to build a culture of shared co-creation and co-accountability in order to maximise the team's potential.

Application: team contract and commitments

Purpose: To establish shared responsibility and accountability for moving the team forward.
Time: 30 minutes.

At the end of every RSC conversation, we facilitate with a team, we explicitly work with co-responsibility and co-accountability for the team agreement by asking the following:

- What is one behaviour or contribution you will make to move this team forward?
- How will you be held accountable for this?

In a Round, each team member has an opportunity to share something specific that they will do, to move the team forward. The rest of the team bears witness to this commitment and participates in establishing accountability. These individual commitments very often illustrate relationship-oriented aspects of what is required by the team at a specific point in time. For example, "I will listen and check for understanding instead of assuming", or "I will temper the number of jokes I make in meetings because I know that too many jokes can get irritating".

Change is a constant process of evolution

Change can be initiated by us, or it can come from outside. Regardless of the size or source of change, it is always preceded by signals or "information packets" revealing what is happening or about to happen in our system (Rød, 2015). Signals can come from

- *within our team system* (internal signals), such as conflict, gossip or poor staff morale; or from
- *outside of our team system* (local signals), such as customer complaints or technology failures; or from
- *the broader environment* (global signals), which would include political change or economic recession.

The main premise is accepting that change is inevitable (Rød and Fridjhon, 2016: 157). It can provide us with opportunities when the relationship system is able to pay sufficient attention to signals of the emerging change. This requires a shared role of leadership, responsibility and accountability to remain conscious, intentional and proactive in engaging change. A new shared leadership process for a new era.

Application: Metaskills Wheel

Purpose: Move a team to action through intentionally creating the atmosphere necessary for change.
Time: 60 minutes.

Amy Mindell (1995) created the concept of Metaskills as *feeling attitudes* that strongly affect our work and our lives. Fridjhon and Fuller (2012) build on this and describe Metaskills as a stance, philosophy or "come-from place" that the relationship systems coach or leader works from to create an atmosphere that will be conducive to the work. These authors masterfully designed the Metaskills Wheel as a tool that a team can use to create a conscious climate for problem solving. We have found this tool particularly useful in engaging teams in change.

We create a wheel on the floor with the challenge of "navigating change" written on a piece of blank paper and placed in the centre of the Wheel. We then populate each of six to eight wedges created by the spokes of the wheel with a Metaskill that would be useful in navigating change. The idea is to explore change through the lens of these different perspectives or Metaskills. Examples of these would be

- courage;
- openness;
- holonic shift;
- inclusivity;
- commitment;
- curious;
- trustworthy; and
- blank (to be filled in by the team).

Metaskills Wheel process and steps to follow

1. Each individual in the group picks one Metaskill they find interesting with respect to navigating change. Have at least two people in each wedge. Before those standing in the wedge speak to one another, ask them to come up with an energetic expression/gesture, in silence that captures the meaning of that Metaskill. Ask them to discuss what this Metaskill means to them, how they have used it and the impact of it. Have them share this with the group.
2. Then, we ask each individual to choose a Metaskill they consider their greatest strength. They physically move into that wedge. Encourage at least two people in each wedge to once again define what that Metaskill means to them, how they could use it to successfully navigate change and to what effect.
3. Each person picks a Metaskill that they find challenging. Standing in the wedge of that Metaskill they define it for themselves, discuss how they could use this more and what its possible impact might be, specifically with regard to navigating change.
4. Facilitate a brief discussion about what each individual has learnt and what might be trying to happen in this team system. Ask how it could be facilitated by taking shared responsibility to intentionally bring each Metaskill and forward the action in the team. This is a powerful tool to reveal the system to itself, to deepen understanding and to build alignment of perspectives to navigate change. This increases commitment to action in the team.

Most teams are biased towards production, typically marginalising the reflection, learning and relationships in the team. David Kolb (2015) tells us that, in order to learn, adults need to reflect on an experience and understand it, before considering how to apply their learning. The willingness to reflect and the ability to learn lies at the core of change.

Putting it all together

Twelve is the maximum number of people to work with when learning this approach. We recently worked with a team of 12 in which there was a great deal of conflict and a lack of trust. Consequently, team members did not work well together and technical performance was compromised. The client wanted our workshop to move toward

- building trust;
- building collaboration and alignment and
- setting a stronger foundation for team effectiveness and high performance.

Throughout the workshop, we used flipcharts to capture responses to questions we asked. These notes then comprised the minutes of the meeting and provided a benchmark for future work. We used the following tools and left plenty of time for rich, real conversations.

Rounds

We started with two questions which were answered in a Round:

1 What most energises you about your work?
2 What is one question you would most like answered today?

Team agreement and expectations (60 minutes)

Owing to the low level of trust, we allowed an hour for this process and focused heavily on behaviour statements that would describe behavioural expectations as specifically as possible.

Further Rounds and small group discussions (90 minutes)

We invited the larger group to work in four groups of three people per group. This allowed team members to answer the questions within their small groups and report out in as a group, in a Round, thereby offering safety and relative anonymity to team members. The questions asked were as follows:

- What is working well in this team?
- What could be working better?
- What are the barriers to the change that is needed?

Metaskills Wheel (60 minutes)

Place tape on the floor to create eight relatively equally sized wedges each representing the behavioural statements in the Team Agreement, with one wedge remaining blank should another statement emerge as important. "Building team effectiveness" could replace the issue of "navigating change" in the centre of the Wheel.

During the discussions in this exercise, it is possible that a new behavioural statement may emerge that needs to be added to the Team Agreement to build team effectiveness. At the point at which this becomes clear, it should be added to the Wheel and later added to the Team Agreement. In concluding the Metaskills Wheel, each team member had the opportunity to start thinking about what they personally would commit to doing differently to forward the action of the team.

Individual commitments in the team (30 minutes)

The questions we often ask to elicit personal commitments are as follows:

1 What can this team count on you to do differently going forward to build this team?
2 How will you and everyone else know that you are doing this?
3 How will you be held accountable for this contribution?

Conclusion

Relationship Systems Coaching and the Relationship Systems Intelligence that lies at its core open up unique ways for leaders and teams to engage. This facilitates relationships that embrace and thrive on diversity and difference and the possibilities these present in teams that are willing to do the work. To succeed, these relationships require shared leadership, co-responsibility, co-accountability and co-creation which provide innovative leadership and team processes for a new era.

References

Fridjhon, M., and Fuller, F. (2012). *Handbook of Organisational Relationship Systems Coaching*. Benicia, CA: CRR Global.

Goleman, D. (1998). *Working with Emotional Intelligence*. New York, NY: Bantam.

Goleman, D. (2006). *Social Intelligence: The New Science of Human Relationships*. New York, NY: Bantam Dell.

Kline, N. (1999). *Time to Think: Listening to Ignite the Human Mind*. London: Cassell Illustrated.

Kolb, D.A. (2015). *Experiential Learning: Experience as the Source of Learning and Development*. Second edition. Upper Saddle River, NJ: Pearson Education.

Mella, P. (2009). *The Holonic Revolution: Holons, Holarchies and Holonic Networks*. Pavia: Pavia University Press.

Mindell, A. (1995). *Sitting in the Fire: Large-Group Transformation Using Conflict and Diversity*. Portland, OR: Lao Tse.

Ness, E.D. (2014). *Learn Or Die: Using Science to Build a Leading-Edge Learning Organisation*. New York, NY: Columbia University Press.

Pollak, L. (2017). *What Are the Different Generations in the Workplace? Your Definitive Guide*. URL: www.lindseypollak.com/different-generations-workplace-definitive-guide/. Accessed March 2018.

Rød, A. (2015). *Endring – systeminspiret ledelse i praksis*. Oslo: Flux.

Rød, A., and Fridjhon, M. (2016). *Creating Intelligent Teams: Leading with Relationship Systems Intelligence*. Johannesburg: Knowres.

Whitworth, L., Kimsey-House, K., Kimsey-House, H., and Sandahl, P. (2007). *Co-active Coaching: New Skills for Coaching People toward Success in Work and Life*. Second Edition. Boston, MA: Nicholas Brealey.

8 The High-Performance Relationship Coaching Model

Sunny Stout-Rostron

A common mistake of executive coaches is to assume the relationship between executive coach and leader happens in isolation from the dynamics of the executive's team and the organisation overall. The coaching relationship is set within the *context* of the team and organisation; it is part of the overall system within which the leader works. This has huge implications for the coach's interventions with the leader, hence my reason for working as a team coach. Below are some *principles* I have developed as my team coaching model evolved from my organisational work and study.

Coaching for meaning

Man's search for meaning is the primary motivation in his life and not a secondary rationalisation of instinctual drives (Frankl, 1946). A key focus in executive coaching is meaning and purpose, and this extends to team coaching. Whitmore (2002: 119) mentions that one of the goals of humanistic psychology is the fulfilment "of human potential through self-awareness". In team coaching, we are working not just with self-awareness but with team awareness, and awareness of the organisation and the overall system. The team needs to determine their overarching purpose in working together, and in essence answer three questions:

1 What is our purpose as a team?
2 How can we develop a shared purpose and shared standards?
3 What will it take for us to achieve significant performance results?

Goleman (1996) cited Maslow as one of the founders of humanistic psychology aiming to understand and help healthy fully functioning people "gain a deeper insight into human nature". Whitmore (2002:

119–220) mentions the five domains of emotional intelligence which are useful to us in team coaching:

1 knowing one's emotions (self-awareness);
2 managing one's emotions;
3 motivating oneself;
4 recognising emotions in others and
5 handling relationships.

For the team coach, the most skilful use of positive regard (Rogers, 1986) is "being present in the moment" (Kline, 1999) enabling the coach and the team the opportunity for "thinking", "change" and "insight" to happen at varying levels of consciousness. The coaching conversation, ultimately, seems to be less about the mechanics of the coaching intervention than the art of integrating pure presence and attention, with the skill of asking the right questions at the right time. It is about awareness that leads to knowledge and action. The team coach's intervention is simply the bridge between reflection, awareness, learning, knowledge and action.

The book *Using Experience in Learning* (Boud, Cohen and Walker, 1996) had a profound effect on my thinking about the team coaching conversation, and the space it opens up for team members to learn from their own experience. In the context of the coaching conversation, when the team members talk about their experience, they are generating narratives that begin to create the present and the past for the team. Storytelling constructs meaning in a different way from merely describing an experience. *Learning, and particularly learning from experience, is therefore a major component of the team coaching intervention.*

Be careful of rigidity – build flexibility into your model

A word of caution – you can be trying to adhere so hard to a "coaching model" that it gets in the way of the relationship with the team, and the personal and professional growth of the team.

Learning from team coaching supervision

The importance of the team coach being coached or in supervision cannot be over-emphasised. As Yalom (2001: 48) says, human problems are "largely relational", and an individual's interpersonal problems will ultimately manifest themselves in the here-and-now of a therapy encounter. The same is true of the coaching environment. The client's interpersonal issues will soon emerge in the relationship between coach and individual client, coach and team client. This was an important aspect of both individual and team interventions, as in Team B we had four coaches working individually with each of the senior executives, complemented by the monthly team coaching.

One of my major learnings was the desirability of having arranged a supervisor for the entire coaching team, including myself and the other three coaches. Organisational dynamics can play out between various members of the coaching team – and, in fact, it can be easy to develop biases and group assumptions within the coaching team if there is no supervisor outside of the coaching team. I tend to play the role of Lead Coach and Lead Supervisor – and that may not be as effective. There is also the possibility of power dynamics between coaches, dynamics between those internal and external to the organisation, and dynamics between the coaches due to personality, seniority, etc. This is definitely a learning for both myself and my co-coaches for future team coaching interventions that we engage in together, and for myself working as a team coach in other organisations going forward.

In previous projects, I have worked with external coach supervisors. In my last study, Team B, I worked with my co-coach as co-supervisors. We had regular sessions to identify our own learning as facilitators of the team coaching sessions, and to integrate our learning back into the next team coaching session. One of our core learnings was to meet with the leaders of the team prior to each team coaching session to be sure that we were aware of what was happening within the internal and external environment, and to incorporate the client's requirements into each team coaching session. This has helped us to alter our behaviours and engagement with the team according to what is transpiring in the organisational environment. For example, managing our own anxiety and trauma from the number of organisational restructurings that took place from the beginning of the team coaching – and to be aware of our impact on the team. There was one major restructuring of the businesses in Client B's Holding Company to support the client operating model. This was followed by a second restructuring in my client company with the introduction of a new CEO and a new operating model to best service the customer sector. These restructurings had a serious impact on the motivation and anxiety of team members.

My co-coach and I grew in terms of developing an "alchemy" between us, being able to co-facilitate without ego or judgement. This has meant paying attention to interventions the other can make that enhances the learning for the team. We have worked together for a number of years and are learning to read each other in the team coaching sessions – and have learned how to intervene when needed in a way that follows as seamlessly as possible from the other. This requires learning to work without judgement or ego.

We also discuss what we did well, and what needs work, after each team coaching session. We have identified parallel processes that we run in conjunction with the team; fortunately, there has been no conflict between us that resides in the team itself. Parallel processes have been things such as not speaking up when noticing or observing bad behaviour in the team that should have been dealt with in the moment (for both coaches and team members). The Team Toxins (ORSC™) exercise ultimately helped us emerge voices and behaviours subtly hidden in the team. This ensures that the team is learning how to listen to each other, and has begun to understand their own limiting behaviours and the impact of those behaviours on the rest of the team. My co-coach and I have learned to complement each other's work, sharing leadership in the room by checking in with each other as we progressed through the five-hour monthly team coaching sessions.

For co-supervision, we met with the core sponsor of the team coaching several times during the process. We shared what we were doing, how the process and outcomes of the team coaching was progressing, and the dilemmas we were facing: for example, the constant organisational restructuring and bullying behaviour in the team. There was a substantial change of leadership in the middle of Client B's team coaching process halfway through the 12-month process. At times, this was very disruptive because the team was constantly having to form, storm and norm. The new leader of the Business Unit had a very different style of leadership to the first. The new CIO was keen to open up even greater robust and open discussion inside the team, and to continue to get rid of the bullying behaviours that took place outside of the team coaching sessions. This has been gradually taking place.

Our core learning as co-facilitators was to deal with the high levels of anxiety in the team and to help them identify blind spots in their co-behaviours – and for us as facilitators to be able to "sit in the fire without catching on fire". In other words, how to sit and be at ease no matter what emerges in the team coaching and together to facilitate a way forward. We could not have done so without meeting regularly with each other, undertaken supervision with our overarching sponsor within the holding company, and staying alongside the thinking of the two leaders of the Business Unit. In future, I will certainly think about engaging a supervisor to oversee the entire coaching team to avoid some of the possible internal dynamics that might get in the way.

Active, catalytic listening

Active listening is listed as a competence (a set of specific skills) which I have restructured as follows: listening for feelings, giving feedback on specific listening skills, giving feedback on the impression team members make on you, paraphrasing; physical listening, reflection, restatement and summarising.

Components of the High-Performance Relationship Coaching Model

My model is four concentric circles (see Figure 8.1). The inner hub is the Relationship. This refers to the network of relationships that are built during the course of the team coaching. The second concentric circle is divided into seven sections, starting with *Contracting*. There are arrows to show movement round the circle. The stages are *Contracting*; *Assessment*; *Diagnosis and design*; *Team inauguration*; *Re-contracting*; *Individual and team coaching interventions*; and *Reflect, review and redesign*. These six stages help to develop *individual awareness, team awareness, organisational awareness, diversity awareness, cultural awareness* and *systemic awareness.*

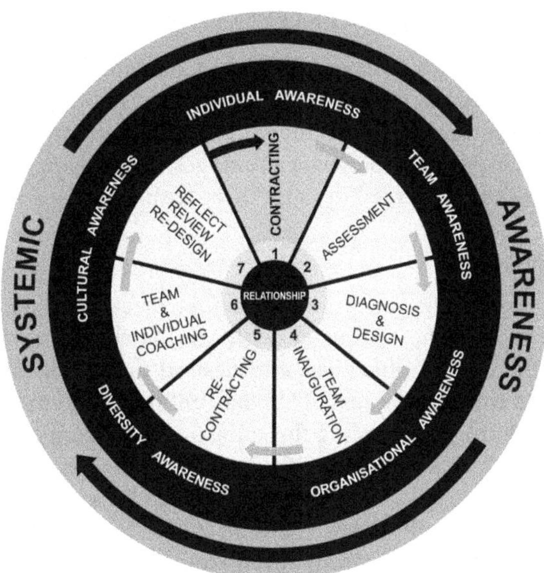

Figure 8.1 High-Performance Relationship Coaching Model.

The components of the model are holistic concentric circles:

- *Inner circle*: Relationship (network of relationships).
- *Second circle*: seven stages of the team coaching intervention:
    1. Contracting;
    2. Assessment – gathering data;
    3. Diagnosis and design;
    4. Team inauguration;
    5. Re-contracting;
    6. Individual and team coaching interventions (five C's) and
    7. Reflect, review and redesign.
- *Third circle*: five levels of developing awareness as a result of the team coaching sessions:
    1. Individual awareness (self-awareness);
    2. Team awareness;
    3. Organisational awareness;
    4. Diversity awareness and
    5. Cultural awareness.
- *Outer circle*: one level of deepening systemic awareness in an ever-widening reach:
    1. Systemic awareness (PESTLE).

The seven-phase High-Performing Team Coaching Model was developed based on the results of three case studies, two undertaken with my financial sector client and one with a multinational media client over a five-year period. Below are the stages of the team coaching interventions as they emerged in these three teams.

Stage 1: Contracting

The initial contracting occurs in your first meetings with the client while determining the chemistry with you as the team coach, and discussing the overall objectives and desired outcomes for the team coaching and for the business. This may entail several meetings with various stakeholders, including the sponsor of the team coaching, the team leader, other more senior leadership in the organisation, and other stakeholders such as direct reports, members of the company's board of directors and the key client or clients. At this stage, you are trying to understand the specific brief from the client to support the team's development. Your work starts here – and you are initially contracting for the *Assessment* and *Diagnosis and design* phases.

In this phase, you are beginning to build the relationship and trust in your capacity to provide the appropriate intervention for the needs of the organisation. It is important to identify the client's goals and boundaries for the team coaching relationship, and to set up expectations for the other phases of coaching. It may be helpful to make explicit to the client the various stages of the coaching intervention, and to get a clear understanding from them about what changes they can expect in terms of skills/competence, attitude, behaviour and performance.

In fact, the coaching starts during the contracting conversations. Success means contracting and goal setting. In these first few sessions, it is important to discuss specific issues where the team and individual members may be stuck. The underlying goal in this contracting phase is the development of the relationship with the client. It requires empathy, willingness to challenge and respect (O'Neill, 2000: 93–97). Here, you try to uncover the key issues, major paradigms and core limiting assumptions within the system, and think with your client about how to address these.

Suggested questions: What do the team's stakeholders require of this team that they are not currently achieving? What is the rationale for team coaching at this point? What is the history that has led up to it? Who is involved in the idea for the team coaching and is everyone in agreement? What other team interventions have you completed previously, and what worked well and what didn't work? What are the "un-sayables" in the team and the organisation? What made you decide to call me?

Overarching learning

My learning from this phase with Client B's teams was that I did not raise enough awareness with the ultimate stakeholder, the client's overarching customer, until our fourth team coaching session when we completed the Team Connect 360°. As we began the first team coaching sessions, the organisation was beginning a series of restructurings, and the team has continued to undergo several different compositions – including a change of leadership at all three levels within the Holding Company. A necessary condition for a successful coaching contract is the willingness of your key team leader to own their part in the patterns at play, and to be receptive to immediate feedback (O'Neill, 2000: 100). I learned the importance of this when working with the Executive Team at Client A, where the team leader was unwilling to be part of the individual coaching process that was aligned with the team intervention. To rectify this with Client B, all leaders had a coach. My co-coach and I also ensured that the team leader's new boss was included in the team coaching sessions. This widened the system. It made a huge impact for the team on their understanding of the wider system within which they work.

Goal-setting interventions

Determining outcomes for the overarching team coaching is important, as are the goals that the team and individual executives achieve during the coaching intervention. The coach is responsible to ensure that goal-setting conversations get the best results. Business goals are about achieving external results; personal goals are what the leader has to do differently in how they conduct themselves to get the business results. Crosby's (1998) three types of goals are useful in team coaching:

1. *Bottom-line goals* – aligned to the reason the organisation exists.
2. *Work process goals* – how the work is accomplished.
3. *Human relations goals* – how people collaborate to accomplish goals.

Ethics in coaching

It is vital from the beginning to clarify the professional and ethical codes that you work to as an executive and team coach. You will find ethics enters the conversation at many times during the entire intervention. This will raise its head with regard to how individual coaches share information about their individual coachees with you as supervisor. It will also appear as you share information about the progress of the team in the team coaching process. Always remember that you can ethically share goals, achievements and areas of development – but never the coaching conversations themselves – outside of the individual or team coaching process, but still within the organisation. It is a golden rule to follow. For me, as a Coach Supervisor in my three case studies, I was very aware of all the dynamics within the teams, but constantly careful not to share that information. Instead, I used the team coaching sessions to help the teams emerge what issues needed discussion.

Peltier appropriately quotes Robert Solomon: "the search for excellence, whatever else it may be, begins with ethics" (Solomon, 1997: xiii, quoted in Peltier, 2001: 222). He explains that executive coaches have to navigate two types of cultures: the business culture which is a proprietary culture based on market enterprise and the individual client culture which cultivates the ethics of care, and where looking after the client's best interests engenders a cooperative culture.

In terms of client intervention, Peltier (2001: 224) suggests the following tips:

1. Develop from the outset clear written contracts of the relationship about confidentiality and boundary issues.
2. Know your limits and practise within those limits and under supervision.

Without having formal, clear-cut ethical guidelines to work from (unlike psychotherapists), coaches need to establish and maintain the necessary ethical norms through their working practices.

Stage 2: Assessment

This is the stage that Hawkins calls *Inquiry*. This second stage is to gather data for the team coaching intervention, and to determine team readiness for the intervention. It is about collecting data and perceptions about the team, their performance, functioning and dynamics; and observing how they interact with each other and with other collectives in the organisation (Hawkins, 2014: 88). This will be revisited in the second contracting once you have collated more data on individual members of the team, and begun to understand the culture of the team and organisation. The assessments are not necessarily psychological instruments at this stage. How you assess team readiness will vary based on the context within which you are to work. All the data you collect together needs to be put into a report in order to write your proposal for the entire team coaching intervention. Also, all data gathered will be needed to co-design the team coaching journey with the team.

At this stage, it is useful to meet with the individual members of the team and have what I call a "diagnostic coaching interview" to get clarity on their job roles, what is working and what is not working for them. Identify how they see their core strengths and areas for development, and what they individually expect from the individual and the team coaching. This gives you time to develop trust with the individual members of the team, and to begin to understand the environment. It is extremely useful to sit in on the management meetings of the team to assess what is working/not working, and what you and they see are some of the issues the team faces. It may be at this point that you are also gathering data to discuss the individual as well as team coaching needs – and to think about the suite of coaches you and the organisation will need to put together for the intervention.

Stage 3: Diagnosis and design

At this stage, you meet once again with the clients to discuss your proposed design for the programme based on client expectations, and your assessment of the team and situation to date. At this point, it is important to contract with the wider organisation – otherwise, you are simply working in a silo of the team itself. This is a three-way contract to ensure you are contracting with the coachee, which could be your sponsor for the team; the representative of the wider organisational system, which ensures that the coaching serves the learning and development for the individual team members; and the leader of the team with whom you will be working.

I was lucky with my contract with Client B, as I agreed a contract with all three key leaders within the corporate holding group. The two key internal stakeholders were the holding company and the umbrella company for Client B. The ultimate external stakeholder was the customer sector. Although at this stage we constantly discussed the ultimate stakeholder for the organisation, the organisational client, we did not bring the client physically into the discussion. My client's focus was initially on the two internal stakeholders.

In this phase, I usually suggest a two- or three-day team inauguration forum prior to the monthly team coaching sessions. I base the two or three days on an individual and team quantitative and qualitative assessment. This may include the Hawkins' Team Connect 360° as well as another quantitative instrument that is for both individuals and the team. The instruments used will be in alignment with the skills, training and competence of the team coach. Following the team orientation, the individual and team coaching sessions are often designed to start.

Part of the Design also includes who will be in the team, who are the recommended coaches for the individual coaching, who the Co-Team Coach will be and who are the core stakeholders that need to be kept in the loop throughout the intervention. Here, I may make clear the various tools, techniques and models that I might be working with during the team coaching: for example, the Thinking Environment® and ORSC approaches to facilitation, Patrick Lencioni's (2002) Five Dysfunctions of a Team, Barry Oshry's (1999; 2007) systemic divisions that lead to organisational dysfunction and the various Systemic Team Coaching applications. The team coaches would also agree the style of facilitation to be used, how the team coaches will be working together and the report-back loops to stakeholders.

My client sponsor was completing an MPhil and wished to work as my co-facilitator throughout the programme. My learning on this programme was how useful it was to have a co-facilitator that worked within the organisation. Although it raised confidentiality issues for some of the team members, she had deep knowledge of the inner workings of the organisation and understood all of the processes at work. At this stage, the two-day team inauguration forum was agreed, and a ten-month individual coaching intervention and a ten-month team coaching intervention were approved. The proposals were written and signed off prior to the team inauguration forum.

Stage 4: Team inauguration

The team coaches will design the team inauguration forum according to what has arisen and been agreed previously with senior management. Usually, it is two or three days outside of the office as a team retreat to initiate, design and launch the team – whether a current or new team. It is a formal orientation of the team. This forum is motivational in nature. The primary purpose is to enhance team effort and shared commitment, with team members learning more about each other, beginning to identify their value-added purpose, starting to clarify objectives, as well as identify core issues that they wished to address in the team coaching interventions. This is where team coaches need to discern the difference between what the team "wishes" and what they in fact "need". This will have become clearer from all of the preparatory work done in building up to the team inauguration. It would even be useful to facilitate a discussion within the team about the difference, as the discussion may help to highlight their own blind spots. In the team inauguration forum,

- team members become oriented with each other and the tasks at hand;
- boundaries are established between team members and non-members;
- individual and collective roles are established and
- team norms are articulated (Wageman, Fisher and Hackman, 2009: 195, cited in Abrahamson, 2016: 22).

In the team inauguration forum, the team creates a Designed Team Alliance which defines how they wish to be together when they do their work. Team interaction is created by agreeing how members want to talk to and act towards each other. What atmosphere do they want to create? What will make them excel as a team? How will they support and challenge each other? What will be their norms for behaviour; what will they accept or reject? It is important that agreements are recorded and referred to on a regular basis (Rød and Fridjhon, 2016: 65). The core purpose of the team forum is to become a team and address how to go forward together – all for one and one for all.

In two clients' cases, I worked with the Strengths Deployment Inventory® on Day One of the team inauguration forum, ending with a Designed Team Alliance exercise at the end of the day. In the third team, I worked with the Enneagram. Day Two was a more qualitative day working with the applications of the Transforming Meetings Methodology to create a forum for the team to address some of the issues that had arisen from the conversations I had with senior management, information gleaned from the initial meetings I had sat in on, from wishes expressed by team members in the individual coaching interviews and from what emerged on Day One of the team forum. In the case of all three clients, the two days started to seriously address the core issues of leadership skill and competence, communication, decision-making, taking action, accountability, diversity and culture, managing conflict, and how to manage the enormous stress and pressures in the workplace.

Stage 5: Re-contracting

Re-contracting can occur as part of the first team coaching session. It can also take place several times during the entire team coaching intervention. It may happen after the Assessment phase with the sponsors of the programme – or again after *Diagnosis and design*. It may also take place periodically between team coaching sessions as the team makes progress and moves through the phases of forming, storming, norming, performing and adjourning (Tuckman, 1965).

This is because, as the Team Coach, you will be meeting often with your sponsor, the team leader and the various stakeholders within the business. At each meeting, you will be identifying "Where are we now?" and "Where do we still need to get to?" As in Hawkins' CID-CLEAR Model, you will be continually *contracting, listening, exploring, taking action* and *reviewing* where you are in the process (Hawkins, 2014: 86). Hawkins emphasises that the flow of the intervention is never linear: you may recycle back and forth into contracting throughout the entire intervention.

What is important is to agree objectives, such as

- a joint view of the current state of the team;
- where we collectively would like the team to be at the end of the coaching process;
- what needs to be addressed and focused on in the coaching work;
- how we need to work together to achieve the most value and
- what the coaching journey map may look like (Hawkins, 2014: 92–93).

Stage 6: Individual and team coaching

In your contracting stage, you would have agreed with your client the structure of the individual and the team coaching interventions. This includes interviews with coaches for individual members of the team, agreed supervision of the coaches (in this case by myself, the lead team coach) – and how the individual team coaching sessions will support the team coaching. The structure and dates of the team coaching sessions would be agreed, as well as the feedback sessions to management in between sessions.

Within the team coaching sessions themselves, there are four stages that I go through in each session. I call it REAL (***R**eflect*, ***E**xplore*, ***A**ction* and ***L**earning*). First is to *Reflect* and review where we are now – particularly reflecting on assumptions that are driving thinking and behaviour. Second is to *Explore* and discuss diverse thinking and perspectives on the issues at hand. This may relate to culture, values, leadership, strategy, decision-making, appropriate and inappropriate behaviours, conflict and communication. Third is to take *Action* in terms of task, behaviour, performance and accountability. Fourth is to define the *Learning* that has been achieved. The process and activities that I use in each team coaching session comprise an integration of Systemic Team Coaching, ORSC and Thinking Environment tools and techniques (Figure 8.2).

In my study with Client B, there was a great tumult during the first eight months. There were two major restructurings. At every team session, someone had been removed from the team due to resignations, moving to new roles or new appointments, and new members added. After seven months of team coaching, we moved from one senior leader to two senior leaders in the Business Unit. One was responsible for integration and operations, and the other for client relationship

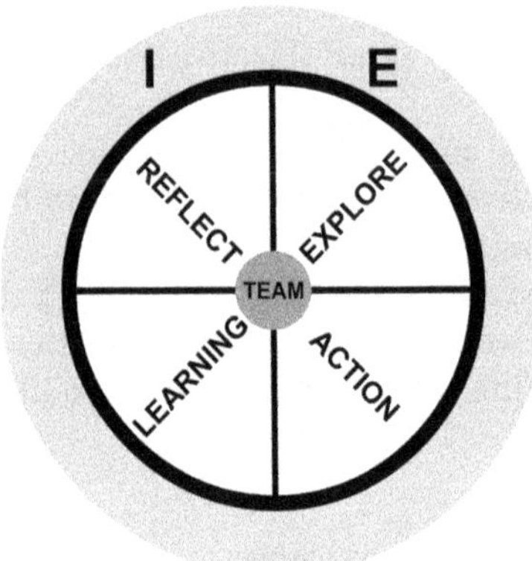

Figure 8.2 REAL Model – structure for the team coaching session.

management. At this point, we identified that there was a need to work closely with the newly appointed CEO of the umbrella company. The constant reformations of the team meant a continual forming, storming, norming and performing.

The coaching intervention – principles

O'Neill's principles for executive coaching are useful in team coaching. Her number one principle is to *Bring your own signature presence to coaching as the major tool of intervention* (O'Neill, 2000: 8–9). The coaching relationship needs to be built on trust (the ability to mutually give and receive feedback); to include the ability to be *present* (on the part of both the coach and the leader); to include a willingness to learn from experience (both coach and leader). It needs to be a highly interactive process.

O'Neill's second principle is that using a "systems perspective keeps you focused on fundamental processes. These forces either promote or impede the interactions and results of the executives you coach" (O'Neill, 2000: 8–9). O'Neill advocates viewing an organisation systemically; she uses a bottom, right-hand Integral Model quadrant similar to Ken Wilber's (2000), claiming it is the largest sphere (including strategic alliances, the global economy, the natural environment and geopolitical shifts).

The third principle is that "applying a coaching method is powerfully effective when you also use the first two principles, bringing your signature presence and using a systems approach" (O'Neill, 2000: 10). One of her essential beliefs is that it is important for the executive coach to embed the "belief that leaders have within them most of the resources they need to address the very issues that seem most daunting". In contrast, Peter Hawkins advocates that the "resources are co-evolved between leaders and their eco-systemic context" (Hawkins, Personal communication, 25 April 2017). Your signature presence as a team coach is what will help reinforce a systems perspective, which will ensure leaders and team members do not get lost in the internal machinations of the organisation.

Stage 7: Reflect, review and redesign

Throughout a team coaching intervention, there are lessons to be learned at individual, team and organisational levels. The team coach learns as much if not more as the team learns and develops. Key questions to ask are as follows: What went well? What did not work well? What were our blind spots? What could we have done differently that would have presented better results? These are all key questions for individual, team and organisational learning. It is important to reflect on these questions after each team coaching session – the coaching will have an impact on the team members, on the team itself, on direct reports to the team, and on the organisation and its wider stakeholders. Such questions are vital so that we do not make the same mistakes in the future.

It has been suggested that "Learning is a process; knowledge is an outcome" (Kozlowski and Chao, 2012: 20, quoted in Abrahamson, 2016: 24). Change and awareness starts with each individual and spreads out through the team, the organisation and into the wider system. Each team member is shaped by the team coaching and the work that is done in between. Leaders within the wider system also learn from the team's cycle and may even be impacted to think differently about their business as a result. Team coaches have a serious role to play throughout the team coaching, which is to facilitate and help the team articulate what they have learned and what they have achieved.

In the team coaching process, the team does not just manage their own transactional, operational and transformation agenda. They are able to grow their individual and collective capacity through learning together. "Good team learning goes beyond the learning of the individuals within the team to the team itself learning, as well as attending to the learning in the wider system" (Hawkins, 2014: 125).

The key purpose of the coaching programme for Clients A, B and C was to develop in leaders the behaviours required to effectively lead self, teams and the organisation to achieve their strategic goals. Throughout the team coaching process, I enjoyed hearing how the team members began to lead their teams differently, learning to develop leadership within their own teams and apply some of the work we have done within their own teams. There have been tears and there has been exultation at various times. Some relationships have been sorely tested. Some valuable team members have been lost to the organisations due to restructuring. However, everyone has learned, grown and developed some level of self-awareness, team awareness and organisational awareness. Without doubt, each team member realises the value they bring to the wider system.

The six levels of awareness

Our state of mind can be influenced by engaging and interacting with others. In the organisational context, a leader's frame of mind can easily influence the thoughts, feelings and behaviours of their direct reports, their team and the entire organisation. Emotions are contagious. When we relate to people we can "catch" emotions that are beneficial or non-beneficial. Neuroscience research shows that the brain actively seeks out "an affectionately attuned other" (Siegel, 1999: 60–63) if it is to learn. Hence, the importance of the rapport developed between coach and client, individual team members and leader, etc. Siegel describes "mindsight" as a combination of insight and empathy. He reminds us that mindsight takes away the superficial boundaries that separate us, one from another, enabling us to see that we are each part of an "interconnected flow, a wider whole" (Siegel, 1999: 58). As a result, we all have a "wish to be part of a larger whole" (Yalom, 1980: 9).

In my work, I have noticed there are five interconnected levels of awareness that have begun to be understood in the team coaching process. They are *individual*, *team*, *organisational*, *diversity* and *cultural awareness*. These are interconnected parts of each one of us. Because the "self" is not fixed but is seen as a process which we continually reinterpret and reshape, we express ourselves through all the facets of our relationships, gradually becoming aware of what is outside of ourselves. These levels of awareness grow as the team grows and develops together throughout the team intervention. The inner hub of the model is relationship – and references the interconnectedness of all our relationships within the organisational system.

Conclusion

Systemic awareness sits on its own, surrounding all of the other parts of the High-Performance Relationship Coaching Model. The development of systemic awareness is gradual and happens as the team members mature throughout the process. As they develop individual, team, organisational, diversity and cultural awareness, they become more aware of their impact on the system overall – and its impact on them. They become aware that their relationships create the network of systems of which they are a crucial part.

In working with the different levels of awareness within the team (individual, team and organisational), each team member gradually begins to recognise the *diversity* in others, developing an understanding of both individual team member's *culture*, and to see the growth of the team culture and its impact on organisational and client culture. As a result, a growing awareness of the *wider system* in which the team operates ensures that the individuals and the team begin to recognise the influence they can have, positively and intentionally on the wider system – as well as the accountability and responsibility they have to the team, the organisation and entire system.

References

Abrahamson, D. (2016). *Team Coaching: Why, Where, When and How*. WABC White Paper, Best Fit Business Coaching Series. Saanichton, BC: WABC Coaches.

Boud, D., Cohen, R., and Walker, D. (eds). (1996). *Using Experience for Learning*. Buckingham: SRHE and Open University Press.

Crosby, R. (1998). *The Authentic Leader: How Authority and Consensus Intertwine*. Eastsound, WA: Paper Jam.

Frankl, V.E. (1946). *Man's Search for Meaning*. London: Hodder and Stoughton.

Goleman, D. (1996). *Emotional Intelligence: Why It Can Matter More Than IQ*. London: Bloomsbury.

Hawkins, P. (2014). *Leadership Team Coaching: Developing Collective Transformational Leadership*. Second Edition. London: Kogan Page.

Kline, N. (1999). *Time to Think: Listening to Ignite the Human Mind*. London: Cassell Illustrated.

Kozlowski, S.W.J., and Chao, G.T. (2012). Macrocognition, team learning, and team knowledge: Origins, emergence, and measurement. In Salas, E., Fiore, S.M., and Letsky, M.P. (eds), *Theories of Team Cognition: Cross-Disciplinary Perspectives*, pp. 19–48. New York, NY: Routledge.

Lencioni, P. (2002). *The Five Dysfunctions of a Team: A Leadership Fable*. San Francisco, CA: Jossey-Bass.

O'Neill, M.B. (2000). *Executive Coaching with Backbone and Heart: A Systems Approach to Engaging Leaders with Their Challenges*. San Francisco, CA: Jossey-Bass.

Oshry, B. (1999). *Leading Systems: Lessons from the Power Lab*. Oakland, CA: Berrett-Koehler.

Oshry, B. (2007). *Seeing Systems: Unlocking the Mysteries of Organisational Life*. Oakland, CA: Berrett-Koehler.

Peltier, B. (2001). *The Psychology of Executive Coaching*. New York, NY: Brunner-Routledge.

Rød, A., and Fridjhon, M. (2016). *Creating Intelligent Teams: Leading with Relationship Systems Intelligence*. Johannesburg: Knowres.

Rogers, C.R. (1986). Client-centred therapy. In Kutash, I.L., and Wolf, A. (eds), *Psychotherapist's Casebook: Theory and Technique in the Practice of Modern Therapies*, pp. 197–208. San Francisco, CA: Jossey-Bass.

Siegel, D. (1999). *The Developing Mind: How Relationships and the Brain Interact to Shape Who We Are*. London: Guilford.

Solomon, R.C. (1997). *It's Good Business: Ethics and Free Enterprise for the New Millennium*. Lanham, MD: Rowman and Littlefield.

Tuckman, B.W. (1965). Developmental sequence in small groups. *Psychological Bulletin*, 63(6):384–399.

Wageman, R., Fisher, C.M., and Hackman, J.R. (2009). Leading teams when the time is right: Finding the best moments to act. *Organisational Dynamics*, 38(3):192–203.

Whitmore, J. (2002). *Coaching for Performance: Growing People, Performance and Purpose*. London: Nicholas Brealey.

Yalom, I.D. (1980). *Existential Psychotherapy*. New York, NY: Basic Books.

Yalom, I.D. (2001). *The Gift of Therapy*. London: Piatkus.

9 Final reflections

Sunny Stout-Rostron

Team coaching – a choice to be a team player

The team coach helps the team to learn from and interpret their own experiences, and to understand the complexity of the environment in which they work. Team coaching works because it is about the results experienced through the relationship between the coach and the individuals in the team, and the resulting team dynamic. It is from this base that the team continues to build their relationship with key stakeholders within the business. It is critical that we identify all the relationships that are core to the business. Gaps are identified in terms of building relationships, managing people, decision-making, executing strategy, communication skills and facilitating meetings. The team will work together in alignment with organisational values and goals.

It is a choice to be a team player. Many of the challenges in organisations stem from our survival-based needs and fears. Some of those needs include belonging, power, independence and control. Our innate fears include fear of failing, of not being good enough, of the unknown and of not being appreciated by others. These needs and fears can exist only in relation to other individuals. They are individual and interpersonal. It is common to witness infighting, competition, and individuals needing to outperform their colleagues and to be acknowledged emotionally and financially. This leads to silo working, an "us versus them" culture, and limiting assumptions, which, in turn, lead to endless misunderstandings, even conflict. But, we are mostly conflict-avoidant, so we bury the problems and are unaware that they show up in behaviour such as sarcasm during a meeting, which can set off a firestorm of other reactions – both overt and covert.

Team coaching focuses on an effective, sustainable and measurable way of developing managerial leaders and their teams. Traditionally, the development of organisations and corporations supported business and performance development models, but ignored the importance of values to individuals, teams and the business – which underpin organisational culture and behaviours. This crucial lack therefore laid the foundation for the development of individual and team coaching – not just for leaders and senior executives but for individuals at all levels within the workforce looking to enhance their professional lives. A team business coach encourages clients to think for themselves and to develop an awareness of their own conscious and unconscious behaviours.

Measuring results

There is no point in developing a team leadership plan in isolation from the rest of the business. If the team coaching intervention is to be successful for an organisation, it is critical to develop a systemic, fully integrated coaching strategy that is in alignment with both the business and talent strategies for the organisation. A vital factor will be to use team coaching to develop key leadership competences aligned with the business and organisational strategy. The team coaching intervention will help each member of the team manage all aspects of transition, transformation and change.

There is a strong link between business results and emotional intelligence (self-awareness, self-management, social awareness and social skill). Team coaching will need to ensure that both the leader and members of the team improve their emotional intelligence skills, which will lead to better organisational performance. This will move the team to balance the needs of the individuals, the team and the organisation. If the team members have grown in terms of self-awareness, the organisation will want to see this "demonstrated" at work: in relationships, management competence, leadership behaviours, emotional intelligence, accountability and performance. Behaviour and performance will be impacted and be measurable. It is behaviour and performance on which you as a team coach will be measured for your success with developing a team.

Conclusion

The core competence we are working with in team coaching is that of learning – and the learning must always start with the coach. This will bring its own rewards in terms of the coach's own individual development and professional success. Every team you coach, and every situation that you confront, will be different and will have unexpected challenges. Yet there are certain universals which emerge. From my experience and research with Teams A, B and C, one golden thread emerges. Your role is to help them to think individually and independently together. With their collective experience, diversity and wisdom, they always have the answer themselves – it's just that they haven't yet found it. Your job is to help them find the answer for themselves.

Appendix A

ExCo coaching interview protocols

Creina Schneier and Anne Rød

High-level organisation diagnostic

1. Where do you want to be as an organisation, and what is preventing you from being where you want to be?
2. What do you think is working well and what's not working well *within* the organisation?

You as a team

3. Where do you want to be as a leadership team and is there consensus?
4. How effective are you as a senior leadership team, and what are your reasons for thinking so?
5. What needs to work better as a leadership team?
6. What do you think the organisation says, feels and experiences about the leadership team – and how do you think they see you as a team?

Yourselves as leaders

7. You – What's your role and what are your responsibilities?
8. You – What is working well for you in your role – and what is not working?
9. You – What's holding you back personally in terms of your own leadership and management effectiveness?

Wider system

10 What are the perceptions of the organisation in the marketplace – and how do you know?
11 What would aid your reputation in the marketplace?

What else?

12 What else if anything would you have liked to have been asked – and what are your thoughts?

Appendix B

Staff coaching interview protocols

Creina Schneier and Anne Rød

1. What do you like and enjoy about working at the company?
2. What is your role and what are your responsibilities?
3. What's working well for you in your role – and what is not working?
4. What does the leadership team do that is effective, and what are your reasons for thinking so?
5. What more do you want and expect from the leadership team?
6. How do you see your career developing – and what help do you need?
7. What else, if anything, would you like to have been asked – and what are your thoughts?

Appendix C

Values survey questionnaire

Creina Schneier and Anne Rød

The senior leaders of your Company would like to review and refine the values that will provide the guiding principles by which you will navigate into the future. This document represents a values survey extended to all staff in the company to ask for your individual input on the values that you experience being lived in your Company – and to ask for the values and behaviours that you would like to experience going forward to ensure its success. After analysing this feedback to understand the values and behaviours that most resonate with all staff, the team coaches will facilitate a workshop to work with the results of the survey, and to help all staff select the core values that will inform how things are done in the Company going forward.

The values survey

Once you have completed the questionnaire, please save it and email it to [email address]. Responses from all team members will remain *confidential* and will be aggregated and summarised anonymously by [the Team Coach]. Your candid, honest answers to each question will be appreciated. Answers to all of the questions should reflect your current experience.

Please complete Questions 1 and 2 by checking one of the response options for each question (click on the check box next to the option you choose).

1 How long have you worked at Company C?

- ☐ More than 8 years
- ☐ Between 6 and 8 years
- ☐ Between 4 and 6 years
- ☐ Between 2 and 4 years

- ☐ Between 1 and 2 years
- ☐ Up to 1 year

2 What position do you hold and what role do you play at Company C?

- ☐ Director/Senior Manager
- ☐ Manager
- ☐ Consultant
- ☐ Technician/Technologist
- ☐ Administrator
- ☐ Other – please specify:

Questions 3 and 4 are open ended. Please answer each question by typing your comments in the text box provided (which will expand automatically to accommodate your input).

3 What are the values you associate with the success of the Company? In other words, what values do you think have made your Company the success it is today? These need not be values you have heard about, but rather the values you think are most relevant.

[ ]

4 Name the four most important values you think your Company should have to be successful in the future. Describe the behaviours required to put these values into practice.

Example

Value: Integrity.
Behaviour: We do what we say and we don't go back on our word.

Value 1:

[ ]

Behaviour required to put Value 1 into practice:

[ ]

Value 2:

[ ]

Behaviour required to put Value 2 into practice:

[ ]

Value 3:

Behaviour required to put Value 3 into practice:

Value 4:

Behaviour required to put Value 4 into practice:

Thank you for completing this survey, your input is valued.

Index

For Product Safety Concerns and Information please contact our EU
representative GPSR@taylorandfrancis.com
Taylor & Francis Verlag GmbH, Kaufingerstraße 24, 80331 München, Germany

www.ingramcontent.com/pod-product-compliance
Ingram Content Group UK Ltd.
Pitfield, Milton Keynes, MK11 3LW, UK
UKHW021425080625
459435UK00011B/155

* 9 7 8 0 3 6 7 6 0 6 5 5 8 *